With many thanks to
Jeannie Taylor and Barbara Martin for their research.
And to the Sunday school teachers
Who helped shape this idea in its beginning stages:
Charlotte Courtney, Bruce and Judy Craft,
Dennis and Peggy Kucera, and Rick Riverman.

Jesus said,
"My sheep listen to my voice.
I know them, and they follow me.
I give them eternal life. . . .
No one can steal them
out of my hand."
John 10:27–28

To God's Precious Lamb:

_____

Given by:

_____

On This Day:

_____

Zonder**kidz**™

The Children's Group of ZondervanPublishingHouse

Editor: Gwen Ellis

02 03 04 / 5 4 3 2

Journey to the Cross

by

Helen Haidle

Illustrated by

David Haidle and Paul Haidle

TABLE OF CONTENTS

NAMES OF JESUS

Messiah, Christ, Savior,

I AM, Mighty God, The Word,

My Lord and My God, Our Savior Jesus Christ,

Seed of a Woman, Seed of Abraham,

Wonderful Counselor,

Teacher, Master, Everlasting Father,

Prince of Peace, Man of Sorrows, Mediator,

Lamb of God, Lion of Judah, Good Shepherd,

Bread of Life, Living Bread,

Light of the World, The Door,

The Branch, Root of Jesse,

The Resurrection and the Life,

Alpha and Omega, First and Last,

The Beginning and the End,

Son of God, Son of Man, Immanuel, The Vine,

Morning Star, The Lord,

God's Holy One, The Rock,

Lord of All, Redeemer, Deliverer,

Chief Cornerstone,

The Way and the Truth and the Life,

Faithful and True, Coming One,

Living One, Bridegroom,

King of Kings, Lord of Lords,

The Amen

In all of history, no other person has ever been
given such names.

Introduction

How would you feel if the biggest army in the world marched in and took over your country?

What if the governor of the enemy army made tough new rules that you were forced to obey?

How do you think your parents would like it if they were commanded to pay taxes to the new rulers?

Would you want to obey all the new laws made by your enemies?

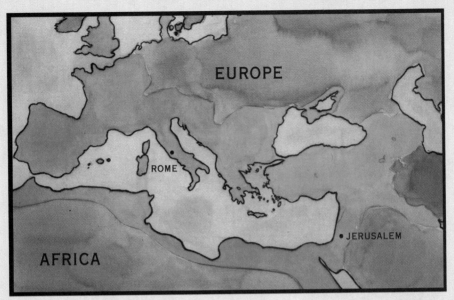

Rule of the Roman Empire around the Mediterranean Sea.

That's what happened to the land of Israel during the time Jesus lived on earth. The powerful Roman Empire had conquered most of the countries around the Mediterranean Sea.

After the Romans won their battles in the land of Israel, they took command over the nation.

The Roman government stationed a large army in Israel and appointed a governor to rule the Jewish people. Taxes were also collected from them.

Anyone who rebelled against the Roman rule was severely punished . . . or executed.

For hundreds of years the people of Israel had been waiting for the Messiah whom God had promised to send.

At the time when Jesus entered Jerusalem on Palm Sunday, the people were longing for this Savior. They hoped he would set them free from the Romans.

Many people believed that Jesus was the promised Messiah. For about three and a half years they had heard him teach and preach. They had seen him do amazing miracles as he healed the sick, the lame, the blind, and the deaf.

Now join Jesus on his final journey to Jerusalem.

Follow him to the cross.

Stand by his empty grave.

Watch him ascend into heaven.

Receive the promised gift of his Spirit.

This journey to the cross and beyond

was the most important trip Jesus ever made.

It was a journey he made . . .

just for you!

Jewish Religious Leaders

Two groups of religious leaders had great power in Israel: the priests and the Pharisees.

Priests were ministers who prepared animal sacrifices at the Temple. They also played instruments and led singing.

The name Pharisee means "separated ones." Pharisees lived apart from other people. They stayed away from anyone they considered to be a sinner.

Pharisees often cared more about obeying every detail of the law of Moses than about loving God or other people. Some Pharisees tried to impress people by standing in public and praying out loud. Many priests and Pharisees hated Jesus.

Here is the story of their plot to kill him. It begins in the town of Bethany, at the tomb of Lazarus.

1

The Plot to Kill Jesus

John 11:1–12:19

One day two sisters named Mary and Martha sent Jesus an urgent message. Their brother Lazarus was ill.

When Jesus heard the news, he told his disciples, "This sickness will not end in death. It is for God's glory."

But even though Jesus loved Lazarus and his sisters, he did not go to their home right away. He waited two days.

Finally Jesus said to his followers, "Our friend Lazarus has fallen asleep, but I will wake him up. Let us go to Bethany."

So they went to the place where Lazarus was buried. Many people also had come to comfort Mary and Martha.

When Jesus saw everyone weeping, he was deeply moved. And Jesus wept, too.

People said to each other, "See how much Jesus loved Lazarus. Then why didn't he keep Lazarus from dying?"

Then Jesus spoke up and said, "Move the stone away."

Martha was shocked! "But, Lord," she said, "Lazarus has been dead four days. It will smell bad!"

"If you believe, you will see God's glory," said Jesus.

Many men pushed and shoved the heavy stone. Finally they moved it away from the opening.

Jesus stood near the doorway of the tomb and called in a loud voice, "Lazarus, come out!"

Something stirred way back in the tomb. Then there was the sound of shuffling feet. And Lazarus hobbled out, still wrapped in burial cloth.

"Unwrap him and let him go," said Jesus.

So Mary, Martha, and the disciples ran to help free Lazarus. As they unwound his grave wrappings, the crowd watched in amazement.

When the jealous priests and Pharisees who lived in Jerusalem heard the news about Jesus raising Lazarus from the dead, they were upset and angry. They wanted to arrest Jesus. So they gave orders that if anyone knew where Jesus was, it must be reported.

"Let's stop these miracles," they said. "More people follow Jesus every day. If he leads them in a fight against our Roman rulers, there will be great trouble! The Roman army will be sent to stop them. And who knows? The soldiers might even destroy our temple— or maybe our whole nation. It's better to kill Jesus than let our entire nation be destroyed."

From that day on, the leaders began to plot against Jesus. "How can we get rid of him?" they asked. "And how can we get rid of Lazarus? People who go to see him end up believing Jesus is the Messiah."

What did Jesus say and do at the tomb of Lazarus?
Why did the religious leaders want to kill Jesus and Lazarus?
Has someone ever gotten mad when you did something right?

"Jesus said, 'I am the resurrection and the life. Those who believe in me will live, even if they die'" (John 11:25).

Jewish Burial

When Lazarus died, he was buried the same day because of the hot climate.

After they washed Lazarus' body, those preparing him for burial clothed him in a handmade burial robe. They wrapped him in strips of linen cloth. Spices and a sticky ointment were spread between the layers of cloth.

Jewish tombs were carved in a hillside or dug in rocky ground. All the good ground was needed for farming. Family tombs had spaces for up to thirteen bodies. As the bodies decayed, their bones were put into stone jars and stored in the corner of the tomb.

Hillside tombs were closed with a huge round stone weighing several tons. Two men could easily roll the stone down a narrow trench, which they dug along the base of the hill. But it was very hard to push the stone back *up* the slope!

Donkeys and Colts

Donkeys were valuable animals to the people of Jesus' day. They carried heavy loads and pulled small plows.

Donkeys are gentle and patient animals. They can be ridden without being trained.

A donkey was known as an animal of peace. It was never ridden into battle. During wars, men chose to ride their fastest horses. By riding a donkey, Jesus showed that he had not come to lead a fight against the Roman army. He had come to make peace between God and people.

About five hundred years before Jesus lived, a young prophet named Zechariah wrote that someday a king would come to Jerusalem riding on a donkey's colt. (A young male donkey was called a colt.)

2

The Journey Begins

Matthew 21:1–9; Mark 11:1–11; Luke 19:29–44; John 12:12–19

Mary, Martha, and Lazarus lived in the town of
Bethany, less than two miles from Jerusalem. Not long
after Lazarus had been raised from the dead, Jesus came
to visit them on Friday, six days before the Passover Feast.
Lazarus, along with his sisters, gave a big dinner to honor
Jesus.

A large crowd also arrived at this time. They had heard
about Lazarus being raised from the dead, so they came to
see Lazarus and Jesus.

On Sunday morning Jesus said to his disciples, "Let's
go up to Jerusalem and celebrate the Passover Feast."

So they started out. On the way, Jesus told two of his
disciples, "Go to the next village. As you enter the city
gates, you will find a donkey tied up. Her colt will be
with her. No one has ever ridden the colt. Untie it and
bring it to me."

Jesus went on to say, "If anyone says anything to you,
tell that person that the Lord needs the donkey. Then the
owner will let you take it."

The two disciples went into the town, wondering what they would find. And they found the donkey and colt standing by a house, just as Jesus had said.

When they were untying the colt, the owner came rushing out of his house.

"What are you doing with my colt?" he asked.

"The Lord needs it," the disciples explained. "And then he will send it back to you in a short while."

So the owner let them take away his donkey.

When the disciples returned with the colt, Peter took off his robe and laid it on the colt's back. Then the other disciples also did the same. After mounting the donkey, Jesus headed down the dusty road toward Jerusalem.

The prophet Zechariah had written about this five hundred years earlier. But Peter didn't remember the prophecy until after Jesus rose from the dead.

Zechariah had said, "People of Jerusalem, shout! See, your king comes to you. He always does what is right. He has the power to save. He is gentle and riding on a donkey. He is sitting on a donkey's colt. . . . Your king will announce peace to the nations. He will rule from ocean to ocean" (Zechariah 9:9–10).

Peter, along with other people in Israel, awaited this promised king. They didn't know that Jesus would rule as king of their *hearts* and not as king of their nation.

Why was it important that Jesus rode a donkey's colt into Jerusalem?
What made Jesus the perfect "Lamb of God"? (*Read next page.*)
Why was it important that Jesus came in peace?

"The Lamb, who was put to death, is worthy! . . . He is worthy to receive honor and glory and praise!" (Revelation 5:12).

The Lamb of God

On this day when Jesus rode into Jerusalem, no one realized that Jesus was God's own perfect Lamb, coming to be sacrificed.

At the beginning of Jesus' ministry, John the Baptist had pointed to Jesus and had said, "Look! The Lamb of God! He takes away the sin of the world!" (John 1:29).

On Passover, hundreds of lambs were brought into the city. They were cleaned, washed, and inspected to make sure they were perfect.

Every family selected a lamb to offer to God. They took the lambs to the Temple, killed them, drained their blood, and offered the blood on the altar.

Families roasted their lambs in large ovens which had been set up all over the city in preparation for the Passover Feast.

Palm Sunday

It was two thousand years ago when Jesus rode into Jerusalem. He was greeted by a cheering crowd and the waving of six-foot-long palm branches. Christians today still celebrate this "Palm Sunday."

Palm branches were like a national flag to the Jews. A palm branch had been engraved on the last coins made by Israel before they were forced to use only Roman coins.

These branches of the date palm tree stood for freedom. By waving palm branches, the people were saying that they wanted freedom from Roman rule.

The crowds greeted Jesus like a king. They shouted, "Hosanna to the Son of David." *Hosanna* means "Please save us!" "Son of David" was another name for the promised Savior. God had promised David that one of his descendants would rule Israel forever (2 Samuel 7:12–13).

3

Sunday: Oh, Jerusalem!

Matthew 21:1–11; Mark 11:1–10; Luke 19:28–44; John 12:12–19

"It's him!" A man's voice shouted above the noisy crowd on the dusty road. "It's Jesus of Nazareth! And he's riding on a donkey!"

The crowds who were traveling to Jerusalem ran to meet Jesus. They had heard about Lazarus being raised from the dead. They knew about other miracles Jesus had performed. The people wanted to honor Jesus as their promised King and Messiah.

Even though people in those days usually owned only one coat, they willingly took off their coats and spread them on the road in front of the donkey. Some people broke off palm branches and waved them.

Others laid branches down with their coats to form a soft carpet on the road in front of the donkey Jesus was riding.

"Hosanna!" they shouted. "Please save us! Blessed is the one who comes in the name of the Lord! Blessed is the King of Israel!" The excited crowd hoped that Jesus would free their country from Roman rule.

When Jesus was halfway down the Mount of Olives, he stopped his donkey. He looked across the valley to the beautiful city of Jerusalem. Tears filled his eyes.

He knew the cheering crowd would soon turn against him. He also knew the time was coming when this city would be attacked and ruined.

Suddenly he began weeping loudly. "Oh, Jerusalem, Jerusalem!" he cried out. "In the coming days your enemies will surround you on every side."

"Your enemies will smash your city to the ground," cried Jesus. "They will destroy you and all your people. They will not leave one stone on top of another."

Tears streamed down Jesus' cheeks. He sobbed out loud as he thought about what the Roman army would do to Jerusalem in the future.

Still crying, Jesus continued on toward the city. No one seemed to notice his tears. The crowds kept shouting praises to him. Their shouts grew louder and louder.

When they entered the city gates, the people of Jerusalem asked the excited crowd, "Who is this man?"

The crowds answered, "This is Jesus! He is the prophet from Nazareth."

Meanwhile the Pharisees fussed and fumed while they watched Jesus ride into Jerusalem. They told each other, "Things are getting worse! Look at how the whole world is following Jesus!"

What did the Jewish people want their Messiah to do?

Why did Jesus weep loudly when he saw the city of Jerusalem?

How do you honor Jesus as the King of your life today?

"LORD, save us. LORD, give us success. Blessed is the one who comes in the name of the LORD" (Psalm 118:25–26).

Did His Words Come True?

The city of Jerusalem was built on a hill. It was also surrounded by a high wall. No one believed Jesus when he said, "Your enemies will smash your city to the ground. They will not leave one stone on top of another."

But in A.D. 66, about thirty years after Jesus was crucified, a group of Jews banded together and fought against the Roman rulers.

So the emperor of Rome sent his son, Titus, to fight Israel. In A.D. 70 Titus attacked Jerusalem with his army. The soldiers broke through the city gates, killed thousands of people, and set the city on fire. They burned the Temple, trying to get some of the gold off the temple stones. Soldiers knocked down most of the city buildings and stone walls. Not one stone was left standing on another.

The destruction of Jerusalem happened just as Jesus said it would.

Temple Sales

The Temple was the only place where the Jewish people could bring their gifts and offerings to God. Visitors who traveled a long way had to buy a lamb when they reached the Temple. (Poor people could buy a dove instead of a lamb.)

Merchants who sold these animals charged high prices. Also, no foreign coins could be used in the Temple, so all visitors first had to exchange their coins for Temple coins.

Money changers had set up tables all over the courtyard. They charged extra fees to exchange foreign money. All of the money changers and merchants made big profits!

Non-Jewish visitors could not go inside the Temple area. They were only allowed in the outer courtyard—a huge area of nearly twenty acres! This courtyard was very noisy. It was NOT a quiet place for prayer and worship.

4

Trouble in the Temple

Matthew 21:12–17; Mark 11:15–19; Luke 19:45–48

After Jesus arrived in Jerusalem, he went straight to the Temple. Hundreds of other Passover visitors followed him. So did Peter and the other disciples.

When Peter walked into the outer courtyard, he took a deep breath and wrinkled his nose. *How can anyone pray or worship here? This place smells! And it's noisy!* He glanced down the rows of booths filled with lambs, doves, and cattle. He heard people arguing about high prices.

Suddenly Jesus stepped over to a merchant's table full of caged doves. Peter watched as Jesus grabbed the corner of the table and flipped it over.

Crash! Clang! Clatter! The cages fell to the ground and broke open. The doves flapped their wings and flew away.

Jesus turned over the tables of the money changers. Hundreds of temple coins and foreign coins fell to the floor and rolled across the courtyard.

Then Peter thought about what had happened three years earlier. Jesus had used a whip to drive the animals and the merchants out of the courtyard (John 2:13–17).

Jesus chased the money changers out of the Temple. He shouted after them, "It is written: 'My house will be called a house of prayer. People from all nations can come there to pray.' But you have made this house a den for robbers."

Peter's heart pounded as he watched the frightened money changers run from the courtyard. What a scene! He looked around at all the priests and their mad faces. But he smiled at the sound of the cheering crowds.

Peter watched Jesus walk quietly among the Passover visitors. He healed everyone who was sick or lame. A group of children gathered around him. They sang songs of praise and called out, "Hosanna to the Son of David!"

This made the priests very angry. They said to Jesus, "Do you hear these children? Tell them to be quiet!"

Jesus said, "Haven't you read about this in Scriptures, where it says, 'You have made sure that children and infants praise you'?" (Psalm 8:2).

The Pharisees frowned. They did not answer Jesus.

Peter sighed. What a day! He would never forget it. Neither would the merchants or the religious leaders. They wanted to get rid of Jesus as soon as possible!

At the end of the day, Peter followed Jesus back to Bethany on the other side of the Mount of Olives. That's where they spent the nights during this week. Perhaps they slept at the home of Lazarus.

What made Jesus angry when he entered the Temple?
What would you have done if you had been a money changer?
What can you do to help make your church a "house of prayer"?

"The LORD says, 'My house will be called a house where people from all nations can pray'" (Isaiah 56:1, 7).

Words of the Prophets

Three times during the last week of his life Jesus told his disciples, "All that has been written about me in the Scriptures will now come true."

Two prophets had written about this event in the Temple many years before it ever happened.

The prophet Jeremiah wrote these words of the Lord: "My Name is in this house. But you have made it a den for robbers!" (Jeremiah 7:11).

The prophet Isaiah had written, "The Lord says, 'My house will be called a house where people from all nations can pray'" (Isaiah 56:1, 7).

Jesus used words from both of these prophets when he chased the merchants out of the Temple.

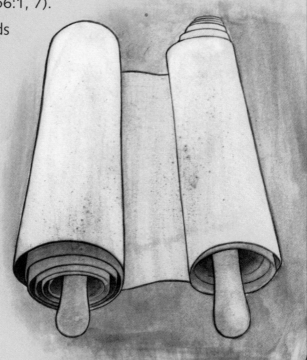

Priests and Assistant Priests

Long ago in the wilderness, God had set apart all the men from the family of Aaron (the brother of Moses). They were to serve God in a special way as priests.

Priests had to wear special clothing as they brought the animal sacrifices and burnt offerings to God. They also burned incense offerings to God.

Then God chose Levi (one of the twelve sons of Jacob) and his descendants to be set apart from the families of the other eleven sons of Jacob. They were to assist the priests.

Levites took turns helping in the Temple. They took care of the Temple building and worked as teachers, judges, musicians, officers, and judges (1 Chronicles 23).

But some of these religious leaders cared more about God's laws than about God. They DID what was right, but their HEARTS were not always right with God.

5

Monday/Tuesday: The Great Pretenders

Matthew 21:18–22; 23:1–33; John 12:38–40

The next morning, Jesus walked back to Jerusalem with his disciples. It was a half hour walk. Jesus was hungry, so he looked around and saw a fig tree beside the road. It was full of leaves, but no fruit was on it.

Jesus spoke to the tree and said, "May you never bear fruit again!"

While Peter and the disciples stood and watched, the branches of the fig tree shriveled and dried up. Peter could hardly believe his eyes. He asked Jesus, "How did the fig tree dry up so quickly?"

Jesus said, "What I'm about to tell you is true. You must have faith. Do not doubt. Then you can do what was done to the fig tree."

Jesus pointed at the hills around Jerusalem. "If you say to this mountain, 'Go and throw yourself into the sea,' it will be done. If you believe and have faith, you will receive what you ask for when you pray."

Once again Jesus took his disciples to the Temple courtyard. There he taught the crowds.

Peter noticed that many of the Pharisees and the religious leaders came and stood nearby. They were not smiling as they listened to everything Jesus said. Peter knew they were upset by what they heard Jesus say.

"Watch out," Jesus warned the people. "Beware of the Pharisees. They don't practice what they preach. They show off by saying long prayers. They only want people to see them and be impressed. But I tell you, God is the one who knows their hearts. And they will be punished for their pride."

Finally Jesus stood up and pointed at the Pharisees.

"You actors!" he shouted at them. "You are like painted tombs—whitewashed and clean on the outside. But you stink on the inside. On the outside you look as if you are doing everything right. But inside you are full of wrong!"

The Pharisees look angry, thought Peter. He could see their narrowed eyes and clenched fists. *They really hate Jesus—maybe enough to kill him!*

"You pretenders!" shouted Jesus. "You nest of poisonous snakes! How will you escape from being sent to hell?"

The Pharisees' faces turned red with anger.

Peter nervously wiped the sweat off his forehead. He knew the Pharisees were mad enough to kill Jesus.

They would probably arrest Jesus if it weren't for the crowds, thought Peter. *But the people would never let that happen. They believe Jesus is a prophet sent from God. By now the Pharisees probably believe he is a son of the Devil!*

Why did Jesus speak out against the Pharisees?

What is a "pretender"? How were Pharisees "pretenders"?

How honest are you? Do you ever pretend to be someone you aren't?

"The LORD said . . . '[Man looks] at how someone appears on the outside. But I look at what is in the heart'" (1 Samuel 16:7).

Painted Tombs

All of the tombs around Jerusalem were painted white before each Passover festival. This was done to help thousands of Passover visitors see exactly where the tombs were.

According to Jewish laws, if you touched a tomb (even if you touched it accidentally), you were considered "unclean." You could not celebrate the Passover or eat any of the feast until much later than everyone else.

When Jesus called the Pharisees "painted tombs," they got upset because they knew it was a great insult.

Jesus was never impressed by how "good" the Pharisees looked on the outside. He knew what they were like on the inside—where it counts. When he called them "painted tombs," he meant they "looked" clean, but they were really rotten and stinky on the inside, just like a tomb full of dead bodies.

The Golden Temple

King Solomon built the first Temple as a very special house for God. But this Temple was destroyed in 586 B.C.

King Herod the Great built the second Temple. He began work on it fifteen to twenty years before Jesus was born. He made it just like the first Temple. The main part was built in only eighteen months, but it took thousands of workers over eighty years to finish it about thirty years after Jesus died.

The Temple and its courts stood on the top of the hill. People in the city could look up and see its cream-colored, marble stones gleaming in the sunlight. One of the Temple stones was thirty-six feet long! And the stones of the tall sanctuary building were covered with plates of heavy gold. Golden spikes also rose from the roof. It was an awesome sight!

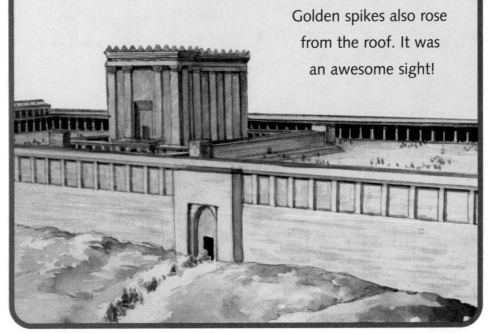

6

When Will the End Come?

Matthew 24:1–4; Luke 21:5–36

Later on Tuesday, Peter and the disciples followed
Jesus as he left the Temple courtyard.

Once outside, Peter turned around and looked back
at all of the Temple buildings.

"Each time I come here, I'm amazed," Peter said.
"The gold-covered stones of the sanctuary are so bright
in the sunlight. I can't look at them without squinting.
And see those huge stones that make up the walls!
They are magnificent. What a building! Nothing is like
it in the whole world."

Jesus answered him, "Don't just admire the beauty
of these buildings, Peter. I tell you the truth. The time
is coming when this Temple will be entirely destroyed.
Every stone will be thrown down."

Peter found this hard to believe. "But, Lord," he
said, "when will all of this happen? And tell us, what
will be the sign of your return? What will be the sign
of the end?"

Jesus gave a stern warning to Peter and his disciples.
"Be careful that no one fools you," he said. "For many will come in my name. They will claim to be the Messiah sent from God. Don't believe them.

"You will hear about wars, but don't be afraid. Nations will fight each other. People will go hungry and starve. Great earthquakes will strike many places."

Jesus also warned the disciples, "People are going to hate you because of me. Many of them will turn away from trusting in me. But stand firm to the end—and you will be saved. The end will come when the good news of God's kingdom is sent all over the world."

Peter wondered, *How long will it be before that happens?*

"Keep watch," said Jesus. "But don't be afraid. For the sun will be darkened. The moon will not shine. The stars will fall from the sky. When all these things begin to happen, lift up your head and be glad."

"Is that when you will return?" asked Peter.

Jesus smiled. "I will come on the clouds with power and glory. I will send my angels with a loud trumpet call. The angels will gather my people from all over the earth."

Peter looked up at the rays of sunshine streaming down through the clouds. *What a sight that will be!* he thought. *Then everyone will know that Jesus is the Messiah.*

What events will happen before Jesus returns?
Why should you be joyful when these events take place?
What can we do to be ready for the return of Jesus?

"Jesus said, 'Yes. I am coming soon'" (Revelation 22:20).

Prophecy of Joel and Isaiah

Hundreds of years before Jesus lived, the prophets wrote these promises from God:

"I will show wonders in the heavens and on the earth. There will be blood and fire and clouds of smoke. The sun will become dark. The moon will turn red like blood" (Joel 2:30–32).

"All of the stars in the sky will stop giving their light. The sun will be darkened as soon as it rises. The moon will not shine" (Isaiah 13:10).

"All the stars in the heavens will vanish. The sky will be rolled up like a scroll. All of the stars in the sky will fall like dried-up leaves from a vine" (Isaiah 34:4).

These events have not happened yet. When they do happen, remember what Jesus said: "When these things begin to take place, stand up. Hold your head up with joy and hope. The time when you will be set free will be very close" (Luke 21:28).

Who Was Judas?

Jesus chose Judas to be one of his disciples even though he knew Judas would betray him. Judas was the only disciple who was not from the area around the Sea of Galilee. He was from a town further south in Judea.

Judas had the job of taking care of the "money bag." This bag held the money people gave to Jesus. Judas bought food and supplies for Jesus and the disciples with the coins. Some of the money was also given to the poor (John 13:29).

After Judas died, John wrote, "Judas was in charge of the money bag. He used to help himself to what was in it" (John 12:6). Did Judas betray Jesus for the money? Then why did he take the coins back? No one— except Judas— knows these answers.

7

Tuesday: The Betrayer

Matthew 26:1–5, 14–16; Mark 14:10–11; Luke 22:1–6

Later that day, Jesus took his disciples aside for a private talk.

"Two days from now will be the Passover Feast," Jesus said. "That is the time when the Son of Man will be handed over to his enemies and nailed to a cross."

Peter was speechless. He had seen Jesus do many miracles. Jesus had fed thousands of people, calmed storms, healed the blind, and raised the dead.

Jesus isn't a criminal. Why would he end up on a cross? Peter wondered. *Besides, the Pharisees and the religious leaders wouldn't dare arrest Jesus during the Passover Feast—it's against the law!*

Peter couldn't understand how Jesus could be charged with any crime. He had done nothing wrong.

At the same time Jesus was talking to his disciples, many of the priests and other religious teachers were meeting together in the home of the high priest. They were determined to find a way to arrest Jesus and have him put to death.

"It's impossible to arrest Jesus during the Passover Feast," the priests said to each other. "All of the people will riot and stir up more trouble! Everyone believes Jesus is a great prophet sent from God."

"But we also have another problem," said the high priest. "The Romans won't allow us to put anyone to death. So we'll have to figure out a way to get the Roman governor to condemn Jesus and crucify him."

Now Judas, one of Jesus' disciples, joined the plot against Jesus. When Judas arrived at the high priest's house, he told the priests his plan.

"I know you want to arrest Jesus. I can help you. I'll take you to a place where Jesus will be away from all the crowds. You can take him prisoner without the people knowing about it."

Judas stood silently and watched the men. When they nodded their heads in agreement, Judas asked, "How much will you pay me if I help you?"

The priests counted out thirty silver coins and gave them to him. (This was the price people paid for a slave [Exodus 21:32].) They were glad to have Judas help them.

From then on Judas looked for a chance to hand Jesus over to his enemies. Judas wondered when this could be done quietly. He knew it had to be a time when Jesus was away from the crowds.

Why did the priests need Judas to help them arrest Jesus?
Why didn't the disciples believe that Jesus would die in two days?
Has a friend ever turned against you? How did you feel?

"Be faithful, even if it means you must die. Then I will give you a crown. The crown is life itself" (Revelation 2:10).

The Death Sentence

The Romans brought their practice of crucifixion to Israel. They nailed their victims to a T-shaped cross through the wrists and heel bones.

In 1968 some bones were discovered in Jerusalem of a thirty-year-old man who had been crucified back in the first century. The man's heel bone still held a large, seven-inch-long, rusty iron spike. Slivers of wood on the nail showed that his cross had been made of olive wood.

Before Roman rule, the Jews had always stoned people as their means of punishment.

If Jesus had lived fewer than one hundred years earlier, the Jewish leaders would probably have stoned him to death.

But now the Romans demanded that every criminal had to be handed over to them for punishment.

The Most Important Feast

Passover is the oldest and most important of all Jewish festivals. It is celebrated every spring as a reminder of the special night when God brought his people out of Egypt.

When the Egyptian pharaoh would not let God's people go, the angel of death was sent to kill all the firstborn sons of Egypt. But God promised that the angel of death would pass over every house where the blood of a lamb was smeared on the doorposts (Exodus 12:1–30).

God told the people, "Always remember this day. . . . You and your children after you must celebrate this day as a feast in honor of the LORD" (Exodus 12:14).

The Passover festival reminds the people of when their sons were saved from death and the people left Egypt to go back to the country God promised them.

8

Passover—Most Important Event of the Year

Exodus 12:1–11, 21–30

The disciples understood why they celebrated Passover, but they did not understand why Jesus would have to be sacrificed for them as the Lamb of God.

The history of the Passover Feast is this:

Long ago, Joseph became a leader in Egypt. He brought his father (named "Israel"), his eleven brothers, and all of their families to Egypt during a time of famine.

The people of Israel grew in numbers as they lived in peace in Egypt. But many years after Joseph died, another Egyptian ruler forced the people to work as slaves.

The people of Israel remained in Egypt about four hundred years. Then God sent Moses to set them free. God kept the promise he made to Abraham.

God had promised, "Your children who live after you will be strangers in a country that does not belong to them. They will become slaves. They will be treated badly for four hundred years. But I will punish the nation that makes them slaves. After that, they will leave with all kinds of valuable things" (Genesis 15:13–14).

When the Egyptian ruler refused to let the people go, God sent terrible plagues to Egypt. Finally God was ready to send the last plague. And Moses told the people to get ready to leave.

Moses said, "Each family must kill a lamb. Put some of its blood on the top and on both sides of the doorframe of your house. The Lord will go through the land. He'll see the blood on the door and he will pass over that house. No one will die in your homes."

Everyone obeyed. Children watched their fathers kill a lamb and drain its blood. Every firstborn son knew—*I will die, unless the lamb dies for me.*

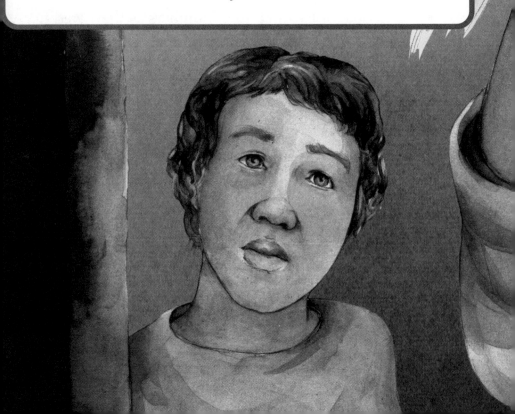

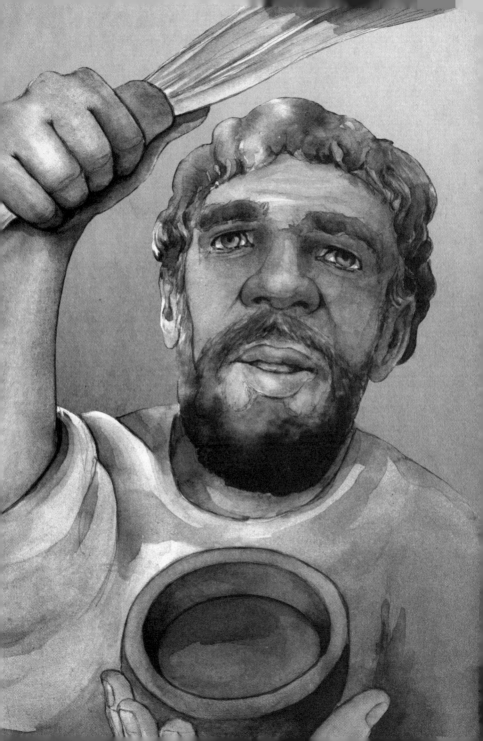

Using a brush made from dried plants, every father smeared the lamb's blood on the sides and across the top of the door of his house.

People followed Moses' instructions: "Roast the lamb. Make bread in a hurry—don't use any yeast in it. Put on your coats and sandals. Get your walking stick."

So the people got ready to leave. They put on their traveling clothes. They set out their walking sticks. After they ate their meal, they waited for the angel of death to pass over their homes. And God showed them mercy— none of their firstborn sons died.

But in the rest of Egypt there was great sorrow. All the firstborn male children and animals died. Now Pharaoh told God's people to leave Egypt.

This was a night they would always remember. Now their journey to the Promised Land would begin.

What made the angel of death pass over a house?
Why did God want the people to celebrate this day each year?
Who is "firstborn" in your family? How would you have felt that night in Egypt?

"Christ has been offered up for us. He is our Passover lamb"
(1 Corinthians 5:7).

The Passover Meal

Roasted lamb is always served for the Passover dinner. But not one of the lamb's bones can be broken. Bread is baked without yeast for that meal. Parsley, hard-boiled eggs, saltwater, and bitter herbs are also served.

The Lord told Moses,"A lamb should be chosen for each family. . . . Put [the blood] on the . . . doorframes of the houses.

"That same night eat the meat cooked over the fire. Also eat bitter plants. And eat bread that is made without yeast. Do not eat the meat raw or boiled in water. Instead, cook it over the fire. Cook the head, legs and inside parts. Do not leave any of it until morning. If some is left over until morning, burn it" (Exodus 12:3, 7–10).

Dusty Roads

Walking was the main way of traveling in the land of Israel. But none of the roads and pathways were paved. Sheep and goats also walked along the dirt roads. Their droppings made the roads even dirtier!

Most people walked with their bare feet. Some wore simple leather sandals. But no matter if people walked barefoot or in sandals, *everyone's* feet got dirty when they traveled by foot.

Foot washing was a special custom and service given to travelers. When people arrived at someone else's home, their dusty feet needed to be washed right away.

It was usually a servant's job to wash the feet of all the guests. Foot washing was a lowly job. It was not a job most people would *volunteer* to do.

9

Thursday Evening: Washing Dusty Feet

Luke 22:7–13; John 13:1–17

On Thursday, the time drew near for Jesus to die. It was also time for all Jewish families to keep the Passover. They would sacrifice the Passover lamb at the temple and eat their Passover meal in the city of Jerusalem.

So Jesus told Peter and John, "Go into Jerusalem. A man carrying a jar of water will meet you. Follow him."

Peter smiled. He knew it wouldn't be hard to spot a man carrying a water jar. Very few men went to the well to fetch water. Getting water was usually women's work.

"When the man goes into a house, find the owner," said Jesus. "Say to the owner, 'The Teacher asks, "Where is my guest room? Where can I eat the Passover meal with my disciples?"' He will show you a large upstairs room. Fix the Passover meal so we can eat there."

Peter and John walked down the dusty road from Bethany to Jerusalem. There they found everything just as Jesus had said. And they prepared the special Passover meal in the upstairs room.

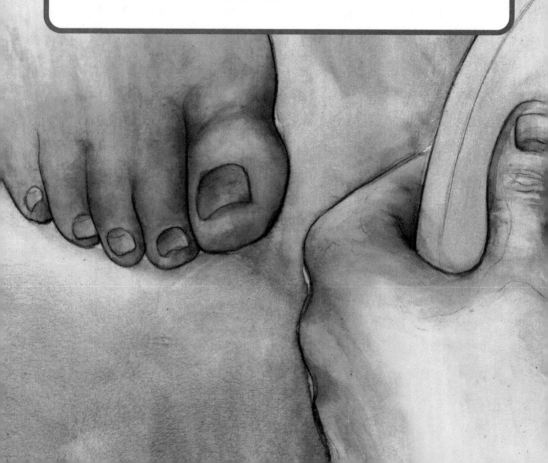

That evening, Peter and the others sat down to eat the Passover meal. But Jesus got up from the table. Peter watched him take off his outer robes and wrap a towel around his waist. Then Jesus poured water into a large bowl and began to wash the feet of his disciples.

Can you imagine how Peter felt? He knew he should be the one who was washing Jesus' feet.

Jesus was the honored guest. But now Jesus was doing the lowly job of a hired servant. Peter's face burned with embarrassment.

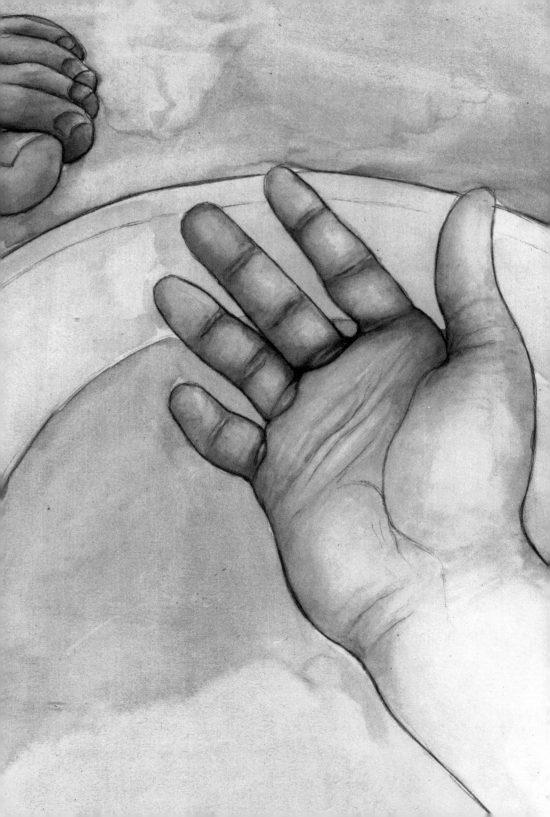

Peter didn't want Jesus to wash his dirty feet, so he pulled his feet away. "No!" he told Jesus. "You aren't my servant. I'll never let you wash my feet!"

"If I don't wash you," said Jesus, "you don't really belong to me."

Then Peter quickly stuck out his feet to be washed.

After Jesus had finished washing everyone's feet, he put on his robe and sat down. "Do you understand what I have done?" he asked. "If I, your Lord and Teacher, have washed your feet, you also should wash each other's feet. I have given you an example. Serve each other as I have served you. You will be blessed if you do."

As they began to eat the Passover meal, Peter thought about what Jesus had said. *Serve each other? Now we'll have to change our whole way of thinking! We will need to stop our arguing about who is going to be the greatest in God's kingdom.*

Why do you think the disciples didn't want to wash each other's feet?

Do you think most people would rather *serve* or *be served*? Why?

In what ways can you serve others around you today?

"The Son of Man did not come to be served. Instead, he came to serve . . . to give his life as the price for setting many people free" (Mark 10:45).

The Great Servant

What does it mean to be a servant? It means to be a giving person who helps and cares for others. A servant is unselfish. A servant thinks about others more than about himself. A servant does the work no one else wants to do.

It takes time and effort to serve others. It is not easy to help your parents or to care for your little sister or brother. It takes time to befriend someone who has no friends.

Jesus didn't come to earth to be honored and served. He came to serve others and to give his life for all people.

Are you willing to be a servant? God will bless everyone who serves. Here is God's promise:

"Serve . . . with all your heart. Work as if you were not serving people but the Lord.

"You know that the Lord will give you a reward" (Ephesians 6:7–8).

The Perfect Lamb

At the time of the first Passover, the lamb a family picked out to be the Passover lamb had to be perfect in every way—no limp, no crooked ear, and no weak eyes. People could not use a lamb they wanted to get rid of. This lamb had to be the best they owned.

After the Passover lamb was selected, it was brought inside the house. The lamb ate and slept with the family for five whole days. Can you imagine what happened?

Everyone learned to love the lamb. It would look at them with its big eyes. It would snuggle close to those who sat on the floor. The lamb quickly became a beloved pet.

It must have been hard to kill the lamb on the evening of the fifth day. They all probably cried. Yet this lamb needed to die—or a member of their family would die.

10

A New Promise

Matthew 26:20–28; Mark 14:17–24; Luke 22:14–23; John 13:18–30

While Jesus and his disciples were eating the special Passover meal, Peter noticed a troubled look on Jesus' face. Peter wondered what was wrong.

Then Jesus said to them, "I'm telling you the truth—one of you will hand me over to my enemies."

All the disciples started talking at once. Each one asked Jesus, "It's not I, Lord, is it?"

Peter leaned over and whispered to John, "Ask Jesus which of us will do this."

John was sitting next to Jesus. He leaned against Jesus and quietly asked, "Lord, who would do this?"

In a quiet voice, Jesus told him, "It is the one to whom I will give this bread." Then Jesus dipped a piece of bread into the dish of herbs and handed it to Judas.

But Judas acted as if he didn't know what Jesus was talking about.

"Is it I, Teacher?" Judas asked innocently.

Jesus answered, "You have said it. Go and do it quickly."

So Judas immediately got up and left the house.

Peter wondered where Judas was going. But then he remembered—Judas was in charge of the money bag.

Maybe Jesus had told Judas to buy something that was needed for the feast. Or perhaps Judas was going to give some money to the poor.

When the meal was finished, Jesus took the bread and blessed it. After he prayed and gave thanks for it, he broke the bread and handed it to his disciples to eat.

"This is my body," said Jesus. "I love you and I give you my life. My body is broken for you. Every time you eat it, remember me."

Then Jesus lifted up the cup of wine. After he had prayed and given thanks, he handed the cup to them.

"Drink it, all of you," he said. "I love you. And I'll pay the price for you. This is my blood of the new covenant-promise. My blood is poured out to forgive many people. Whenever you drink it, remember me."

Peter silently ate the bread. And he drank from the cup that was passed around the table. Many questions ran through his mind. How would Jesus' body be broken? How would his blood be poured out?

Peter still did not understand what Jesus meant about suffering and dying. Peter wondered, *Why will we have to "remember" him? Is he going to leave us?*

What did Jesus say about the bread and the cup?

How is Jesus like the Passover lamb?

What does the "Lord's Supper" or "Holy Communion" mean to you?

"When you eat the bread and drink the cup, you are announcing the Lord's death until he comes again" (1 Corinthians 11:26).

Covenant-Testament

Jesus said, "This cup is my blood of the new covenant [testament]."

Today Christians still celebrate this "Last Supper." It is called "Holy Communion" or the "Lord's Supper." It is a time to be close to Jesus, to pray to him, and to remember all that he has done for us.

People today also write out their "last will and testament." A will is made *before* someone dies. The writer of the will makes decisions about what other people will receive. The will goes into effect *after* the person dies. People often pay a high price to make their will and testament.

Jesus paid a high price for his testament agreement. It was the highest price of all—his life!

And now we can receive the greatest gift—Jesus himself and all his love and forgiveness.

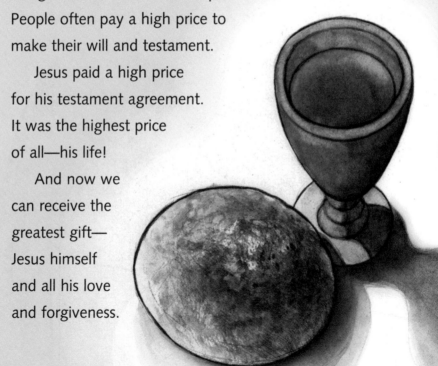

The Last Few Hours

What did Jesus do when he knew he had only a few more hours to live? He spent time with his friends.

Jesus wanted to prepare them for his death. And he wanted to share some special thoughts before he left them.

If you knew you only had a few hours to live, what would you do? What would you want to tell your family and friends? What would you say to your mom? Your dad? Your best friend?

You would probably want to spend time with the people you loved the most. You would take time to share your thoughts with them. And you would tell them how special they have been to you.

11

Little Time Left

John 14–16

After Jesus and his disciples finished the Passover meal, they sang the Passover hymn: "Give thanks to God, for he is good. His love goes on forever."

Peter wished this moment would never end. He felt very close to Jesus and the other disciples. He didn't want to leave the room.

Jesus seemed to understand the closeness of the moment. "I am the true vine," he told them. "All of you are like branches that grow in me and from me. That's how close we are to each other."

Looking around at each of his disciples, Jesus said, "Stay close to me. No branch can bear fruit by itself. It must be connected to the vine."

Jesus held up a small bunch of grapes left from the meal and explained, "If you live in me and I live in you, then you will be fruitful. Let my life flow through you. Then your lives will be full of love and kindness. Always remember: I am the vine. You are the branches. You can't produce any fruit without me."

Then Jesus got up to leave. Peter and the others followed him outside to the streets and finally out the city gate. The full moon lit up the pathway to the brook at the bottom of the hill.

Peter walked by himself, deep in thought. He did not even hear the crickets chirping their night song. Suddenly Peter felt a warm hand on his shoulder.

"Don't be worried," Jesus told him. "Trust in God. And trust in me also."

As Peter looked around, he noticed worried looks on the other disciples' faces as well.

Jesus saw their worried faces, too. He said to them, "Remember what I told you? Even though I am going away, you won't be left alone. I will ask my Father to send you the Holy Spirit. The Spirit will help you remember everything I have told you. And he will never leave you."

Reaching the brook, they all crossed over it and then headed up the Mount of Olives.

Moonlight lit up Jesus' face as he said, "A time is now coming when you will all leave me. But I am not really alone. My heavenly Father is always with me."

Peter frowned as he thought, *I'm not going to leave Jesus . . . no matter what he says.*

"I have warned you about what will happen," said Jesus. "Don't be upset or worried. I give you my peace. In this world you will have trouble. But cheer up! Be brave. I have won the battle. And I give you the victory!"

Why did Jesus tell his disciples that they would all leave him?

How is Jesus like a vine? How are you like a branch?

How are you (a branch) staying close to Jesus (the vine)?

"Jesus said, 'I leave my peace with you. I give my peace to you. . . . Do not let your hearts be troubled. And do not be afraid'" (John 14:27).

Vines and Branches

Vineyards grow in many places throughout the land of Israel. The roots of a grapevine go down deep into the soil. The vine carries food and water from the ground to the branches. If any branch breaks off or is cut off from the vine, it will die. The separated branch has no other way to get its own food and water.

Tree branches that break off will also die. But these branches can still be used for something like carving or for making furniture. Jesus knew this because he had worked as a carpenter.

But when any branch breaks off a *vine*, it will not only die, but it will be good for nothing. Broken vine branches are totally useless. The only thing you can do with them is to burn them in a fire.

The Good Shepherd

A good shepherd always protects his sheep. Even in times of danger, a good shepherd never runs away.

Jesus said, "The good shepherd gives his life for the sheep. But the hired man is not the one who owns the sheep. So when the hired man sees the wolf coming, he leaves the sheep and runs away. Then the wolf attacks the flock and scatters it. The hired man runs away because he is just a hired man. He does not care about the sheep.

"I am the good shepherd," said Jesus. "I know my sheep, and my sheep know me. . . . I give my life for the sheep. . . . No one takes my life from me. I give it up.

"My sheep listen to my voice. . . . They follow me. I give them eternal life, and they will never die. No one can steal them out of my hand" (John 10:11–15, 17, 18, 27–28).

12

Thursday before Midnight: In the Garden

Matthew 26:31–46; Mark 14:27–42; Luke 22:39–46

Peter walked silently beside Jesus as they came to the Garden of Gethsemane.

Jesus said, "Tonight you will all run away. It is written in the Scriptures, 'I will strike the shepherd down. Then the sheep will be scattered'" (Zechariah 13:7).

"No!" Peter protested. He refused to believe this would happen. "The others may turn away, but I never will!" he said. And all the other disciples said the same thing.

Placing his hand gently on Peter's arm, Jesus said, "It's the truth, Peter. Before the rooster crows at dawn, you will say three times that you don't know me."

Grabbing Jesus by the arm, Peter insisted, "I may have to die with you. But I will never say that I don't know you!" Peter saw tears in Jesus' eyes. But Jesus was silent.

When they entered the garden, Jesus said to them, "Sit down here while I go to pray." But he took Peter, James, and John farther into the garden with him.

Peter could see how sad and troubled Jesus looked.

"What is wrong, Master?" asked Peter. He could see that Jesus was in great pain.

"My soul is very sad," Jesus said in a hushed voice. "I feel close to death."

The three disciples silently followed Jesus deeper into the garden. Finally Jesus stopped.

"Stay here," he said. "Keep watch with me." He walked farther, then fell with his face to the ground.

Peter listened as Jesus prayed, "My Father. You can do anything. Take this pain and sorrow away from me. But let what you want be done, not what I want."

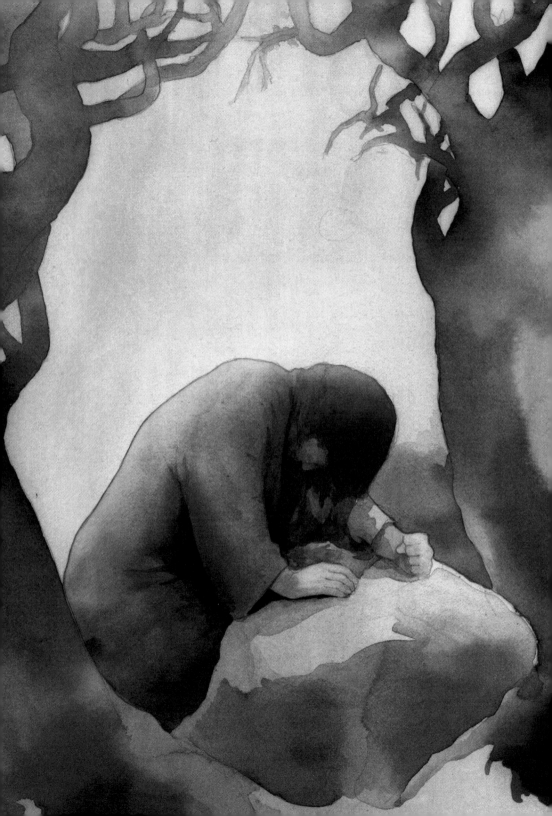

Peter tried to stay awake and pray, but he was too tired. A short while later, Peter tried to open his eyes when Jesus returned. He heard Jesus say, "Peter, couldn't you watch with me for one hour? Watch and pray!"

Again Jesus prayed. Again Peter and the others slept.

The third time Jesus prayed, God sent an angel from heaven to strengthen him. Then Jesus prayed even harder. He knew what was going to happen that night. He knew the suffering ahead of him. His sweat fell to the ground like great drops of blood.

Once again Peter felt Jesus shake him awake.

"Get up!" Jesus said to him. "Now it is time for me to be handed over to my enemies."

Suddenly Peter heard the noise of an angry crowd. His heart pounded. He sat up and looked toward the garden entrance. A large group of people carrying torches had entered the garden and were heading right toward Jesus!

What did Jesus ask his heavenly Father to do?

Why do you think God sent an angel to Jesus in the garden?

What is the hardest or most painful thing you have ever done?

"Jesus said, 'Watch and pray. Then you won't fall into sin when you are tempted'" (Matthew 26:41).

Did Angels Help Jesus?

"All angels are spirits who serve" (Hebrews 1:14).

Did angels ever come to serve Jesus? Yes—once in the wilderness and also in the garden.

After his baptism, Jesus went to the mountains in the desert wilderness. He did not eat any food for forty days and nights. Then the Devil came to tempt Jesus. After Jesus resisted every temptation, the Devil left him. Then "angels came and took care of him" (Matthew 4:11). We do not know how the angels took care of Jesus. Maybe they also brought him food or water.

Another angel strengthened Jesus just before he was arrested in the Garden (Luke 22:43). We don't know exactly what this angel did. We do know that Jesus needed more strength to face the suffering that lay ahead of him.

The Garden

The Garden of Gethsemane was a grove of olive trees on the lower slope of the Mount of Olives. Jesus and his disciples often met there.

The name "Gethsemane" means "oil press." A large, stone oil press probably stood in the garden. An oil press was made out of two very heavy stones.

Olives were poured on top of one of the stones. The other stone was pressed down on top of the olives. When the olives were crushed, oil poured out. The oil ran down long grooves in the rock into a bowl at the bottom.

When Jesus prayed in the Garden of Gethsemane, the load of the world's sin "pressed" down on him. But Jesus didn't run away from death on the cross. He chose to suffer for our sin so we could be forgiven.

13

Thursday around Midnight: Arrested!

Matthew 26:47–56; Mark 14:43–50; Luke 22:47–53; John 18:1–12

An angry, shouting crowd shattered the silence of the garden. Peter saw many soldiers, along with a mob sent by the priests and Pharisees. By the light of their torches, Peter could see swords and clubs that they carried.

What are they doing here? wondered Peter. *They can't arrest Jesus! It's illegal to arrest anyone at night. And what is Judas doing with them?*

Judas was walking at the front of the mob. He led them over to Jesus. Now, Judas had arranged a signal with the guards. He told them, "You can arrest the one whom I kiss." So he went to Jesus and said, "Greetings, Teacher!" Then he kissed Jesus.

Jesus already knew everything that was going to happen. So he said, "Judas, are you handing me over with a kiss?" Then Jesus stepped toward the crowd of soldiers and asked, "Who is it that you want?"

"Jesus of Nazareth," they answered.

"I AM he," said Jesus.

When Jesus spoke those words, the soldiers and the crowd quickly moved away from him. They stumbled backward and fell to the ground.

"I told you I AM he," Jesus repeated. "Am I leading a band of armed men against you? Do you have to come out with swords and clubs to capture me? But this has happened so the words of the prophets will come true."

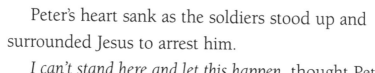

Peter's heart sank as the soldiers stood up and surrounded Jesus to arrest him.

I can't stand here and let this happen, thought Peter. Yanking out his sword, he rushed at the angry mob. He swung his sword wildly and cut off the ear of the high priest's servant named Malchus.

The servant screamed in pain!

"Stop it!" Jesus told Peter. "I will take the suffering my Father gives me." Bending down, Jesus picked up the servant's ear, put it back on his head, and healed it. Everyone stared in amazement!

"Put away your sword, Peter," said Jesus. "Don't you know I can ask my heavenly Father for help? He would send twelve legions [armies] of angels to my rescue. But all this has happened so the Scriptures will come true."

No one said a word. Then the soldiers grabbed Jesus and tied his hands. Peter dropped his sword and ran. The other disciples followed him into the darkness of the garden.

Peering from behind a tree, Peter watched the soldiers lead Jesus out of the garden. He wondered, *Why didn't Jesus let me fight the mob? And why didn't he use his power to escape? Now what will they do with him?*

Why didn't Jesus let his disciples fight for him?

Why didn't Jesus ask God to send the heavenly armies?

When have you wondered why God allowed hard times in your life?

"Jesus said, 'The reason my Father loves me is that I give up my life. . . . No one takes it from me. I give it up myself'" (John 10:17–18).

The Powerhouse Army

Do you think it was easy for Jesus to die for us?

As a man, Jesus had feelings just like all people—love, joy, pain, hunger, anger, and deep sorrow.

A few hours before his arrest, Jesus felt deeply upset. He knew the terrible pain and death he was going to suffer. He could have escaped from the soldiers who came to arrest him. He could have asked his heavenly Father to send a powerful angel army to defend him and fight for him.

One "legion" of the Roman army numbered about 6,000 soldiers. Jesus said he could have asked for an army of *twelve* legions of angels! Wow! What an army!

Once, long before Jesus lived, King Sennacherib of Assyria came to attack Jerusalem. It took only ONE of God's angels to destroy Assyria's entire army of 185,000 soldiers (2 Kings 19:35).

What could an army of over 70,000 angels have done to help Jesus?

The Jewish Court

The Jewish court of justice was called the Sanhedrin. It consisted of seventy men. The high priest was president. This court was known throughout the world for its excellent laws. Read these laws and see if you can find any that were broken during the trial of Jesus.

1. No one could be arrested at night.
2. All trials were to be open to the public.
3. Trials were not to be held during feast days or on the Sabbath.
4. Trials were to be held in the Hall of Hewn Stone at the Temple.
5. The accused person was not to be questioned without someone to defend him.
6. Persons on trial were to be treated with respect—no hitting or spitting.
7. Men of the jury were to consider each trial for two or three days (with one day being a day of fasting).
8. Only acquittals could be made on the same day as the trial. Condemnations required a two-day trial.
9. Jurors were to vote individually (from youngest to eldest). No "group" voting was allowed.

14

Friday—Midnight to Morning: On Trial

Matthew 26:57–68; Mark 14:53–65; John 18:19–23

After the guards arrested Jesus, they took him to the house of the high priest. Members of the Jewish court were waiting there to put Jesus on trial.

The priests and the whole court were trying to find some false witnesses who would testify against Jesus. They needed evidence so they could condemn Jesus.

Members of the court listened as the priests brought many witnesses who spoke against Jesus. But all of the witnesses lied. Their stories did not agree.

At last some men stood up and said, "We heard Jesus say, 'I will destroy this Temple that is made with hands, and in three days I will build another, not made with hands.'" But even these men couldn't agree about what Jesus had said.

Finally the high priest pointed his finger at Jesus and asked, "Aren't you going to answer these charges? What do you have to say for yourself?"

Jesus said nothing.

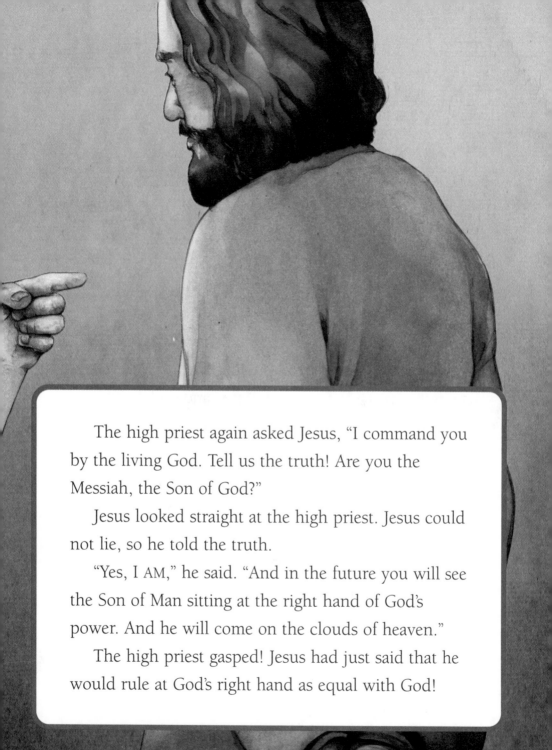

The high priest again asked Jesus, "I command you by the living God. Tell us the truth! Are you the Messiah, the Son of God?"

Jesus looked straight at the high priest. Jesus could not lie, so he told the truth.

"Yes, I AM," he said. "And in the future you will see the Son of Man sitting at the right hand of God's power. And he will come on the clouds of heaven."

The high priest gasped! Jesus had just said that he would rule at God's right hand as equal with God!

The high priest clenched his fists. Grabbing the front of his robe, he yanked hard. He ripped his robe down the front to show how upset and angry he was.

"Why do we need any more witnesses?" he shouted to the jury. "You have all heard this blasphemy against God. What do you think?"

Instead of taking time to consider the verdict, the men of the jury jumped up and shouted, "He is guilty! He deserves to die!"

Some of the men spit on Jesus. Others blindfolded him, then slapped him and hit him with their fists. The guards also beat him. They all mocked Jesus and said, "If you are the Messiah, you know everything. Tell us who hit you!"

Only two men on the jury did not agree with this trial. But no one would listen to either one of them. Their names were Nicodemus and Joseph of Arimathea.

What did Jesus say that upset the high priest and the jury?

Why didn't the Jewish court give Jesus a fair trial?

Have you ever been accused of something you didn't do? How did you feel? How do you think Jesus felt?

"Lambs are silent while their wool is being cut off. In the same way, he didn't open his mouth" (Isaiah 53:7).

The Great "I AM"

Hundreds of years earlier, God had spoken to Moses from a burning bush. God had told Moses to bring all the Jewish people of Israel out of Egypt. God had said, "I AM WHO I AM. Here is what you must say to the Israelites. Tell them, 'I AM has sent me to you'" (Exodus 3:14).

Jewish law stated that anyone who made himself equal with God ("I AM") was guilty of blasphemy. That person would be put to death by stoning.

The high priest had asked, "Are you the Son of God?" So when Jesus said, "I AM," he was claiming to be the Messiah. To the Jewish leaders, this was "blasphemy."

But what if Jesus' words were true? What if he *was* the Son of God?

The council didn't stop to think that Jesus might be telling the truth. They were so sure he was lying.

Simon Peter

Simon (Peter) worked as a fisherman at the Sea of Galilee. One day Jesus called to him and said, "Come. Follow me. I will make you a fisher of people." At once Simon left his nets and followed Jesus (Matthew 4:18–20). Jesus changed Simon's name to "Peter," which means "Rock" (John 1:42).

Peter was the leader of the twelve disciples. He was quick to speak and quick to act. He was the one who walked on the water to Jesus. He tried to defend Jesus in the garden. Jesus healed Peter's mother-in-law when she was sick with a fever (Matthew 8:14–15). Later Peter took his wife on his travels (1 Corinthians 9:5). The Bible doesn't tell us what happened to Peter. But tradition says that Peter and his wife died as martyrs for their faith in Jesus.

15

I Don't Know Him!

Matthew 26:69–75; Mark 14:66–72; Luke 22:54–62; John 18:15–27

Peter was leaving the garden when he suddenly heard footsteps behind him. *Someone's following me! Will I be arrested, too?* He turned quickly and saw a man running toward him in the moonlight.

When he recognized John, he sighed with relief. Together they followed far behind the crowd of men who took Jesus back to Jerusalem.

"Where do you think they're going?" asked John.

Peter pointed to a big building up ahead. "The high priest's house," he said. They saw the crowd go in the gate.

The two friends hid near the gate and watched the soldiers build a fire in the middle of the courtyard.

"Wait here," whispered John. "I know some of the people who work for the high priest."

Peter watched him enter the courtyard. A little later he saw John speak to the woman on duty at the gate. Then John motioned for Peter to come inside.

When Peter came through the gate, the woman looked at him and said, "You also were with Jesus of Galilee."

Peter broke out in a cold sweat. "No! I was not," he said. He hurried over to warm himself by the fire.

One of the servants saw Peter's face in the firelight. She pointed to him and said, "This man was with Jesus."

Peter's heart pounded with fear. He told her firmly, "Woman, I don't know the man."

Later, along toward morning, another servant spoke up. "You must have been one of them," he said to Peter. "The way you talk gives you away. You sound just like someone from Galilee."

This man was a relative of Malchus, the servant whose ear Peter had cut off earlier that evening. The man looked more closely at Peter and asked him, "Didn't I just see you with Jesus in the olive grove?"

Peter cursed and swore as he protested, "Man, I don't know what you're talking about!"

When Peter finished saying these words, he heard a rooster crow. He looked up and saw the soldiers leading Jesus out of the high priest's house. Jesus looked across the courtyard. His eyes met Peter's.

Then Peter remembered what Jesus had said to him: "Before the rooster crows at dawn, you will say three times that you don't know me."

Peter turned and rushed out of the courtyard gate. He broke down and sobbed. "Earlier I ran away when they arrested Jesus. Now I've denied him. Oh, God, forgive me!"

Why did Peter deny that he knew Jesus?

How was Peter's sadness different from the sadness Judas felt?

When have you denied being a Christian by what you said or did?

"Jesus said, 'What about those who say in front of others that they know me? I will also say in front of my Father who is in heaven that I know them'" (Matthew10:32).

Judas Is Sorry

Like Peter, Judas also was very sorry that he betrayed Jesus. When he found out that the Jewish court had sentenced Jesus to die, he decided to return the thirty silver coins. He hurried to the Temple and found the priests.

"I have sinned," said Judas. "I handed over a man who is not guilty."

"What do we care?" the priests answered. "That's your problem, not ours."

Judas threw the coins at them and left. Then he went out and hanged himself.

The priests picked up the money, but they couldn't put it in the Temple treasury. It was "blood money" (money paid to arrest a criminal who would be killed). So they used it to buy a potter's field. The field became a burial ground for foreigners who died in Israel and who could not be taken back to their homeland (Matthew 27:1–10).

Pontius Pilate

The Roman emperor sent Pontius Pilate to be governor over Israel in about A.D. 25. Pilate was governor during the time of Jesus' ministry. Pilate lived in another city in Israel, but he went to Jerusalem during the Jewish feasts.

As the Roman governor, Pilate was in charge of keeping law and order in Israel. All criminals who deserved death had to be sent to Pilate for judgment. While Pilate was judging Jesus, his wife sent him an urgent message.

"Don't have anything to do with that man," she wrote. "He is not guilty. I have suffered a great deal in a dream today because of him" (Matthew 27:19).

Pilate felt his wife's dream was important. He agreed with her that Jesus was innocent.

But Pilate was afraid of the angry mob. He knew that if they complained about him to Rome, he could lose his job.

16

At Dawn Friday Morning— He Must Die!

Matthew 27:11–14; Mark 15:1–5,; Luke 23:1–25; John 18:28–37

Pontius Pilate watched the Passover crowds from his window. He worried about fights breaking out this week.

He was deep in thought when a Roman officer came to his room and said, "Governor, some Jewish priests are in the courtyard. They have brought a special prisoner for you to judge. They want to talk to you, but they can't come inside because this isn't a Jewish building."

Pilate walked out to the courtyard, where the priests waited with their prisoner. Pilate noticed dried blood and bruises on the prisoner's face and neck.

"This criminal tells people not to pay taxes," said the priests. "He is guilty of making trouble all over our land."

Pilate listened to them tell lies about Jesus. "Go away," Pilate told them. "Don't bother me with this man. You judge him according to your laws."

"But he should be put to death," said the priests. "And since we are not allowed to execute anyone, you must be the one to sentence him. Jesus must be punished—he claims to be a king!"

All the while the priests accused Jesus, he was silent. He didn't say one word.

Pilate was amazed at this. He asked Jesus, "Aren't you going to defend yourself? See how many crimes they charge you with."

Jesus still said nothing. So Pilate took him alone inside the judgment hall for questioning. He asked Jesus, "Are you the king of the Jews?"

"Yes," Jesus said quietly. "But my kingdom is not part of this world."

Jesus said, "If my kingdom were of this world, those who serve me would fight for me. They would keep me from being arrested. My kingdom is from another place."

After talking to Jesus, Pilate knew he was innocent. Going back outside, Pilate told the priests, "I don't think this man deserves to die."

The priests protested. "But he makes trouble wherever he goes! According to our laws, he must die!"

When Pilate found out that Jesus was from Galilee, he decided to send Jesus to Herod, the Jewish king over that area. Herod was staying in Jerusalem during Passover.

Herod had heard about Jesus. He was glad to see Jesus in person. He hoped that Jesus would perform one of his miracles. But when Herod questioned Jesus, he never said a word. Finally Herod and the soldiers dressed him up like a king and made fun of him. A short time later Herod sent Jesus back to Pilate.

Why didn't Pilate want to condemn Jesus to die?

Why did Jesus call himself a "king"? What kind of a king was he?

When have you been afraid of what other people would say or do?

"Jesus was the first to rise from the dead. He rules over the kings of the earth" (Revelation 1:5).

King of the Jews

The first people to call Jesus "the king of the Jews" were the wise men who traveled to Israel from the East. When they arrived in Jerusalem, they asked, "Where is the child who has been born to be king of the Jews? When we were in the east, we saw his star. Now we have come to worship him" (Matthew 2:2).

This news was not welcomed by Herod the Great, who reigned as king of the Jews from 40–4 B.C. In fact, Herod was very upset. He found out from the wise men when the star had appeared. Then he ordered that all little boys in Bethlehem who were two years old and under should be killed. (Read this story in Matthew 2:13–18.)

The king who ruled in Israel during the time of Jesus' ministry and crucifixion was King Herod Archelaus. He was the son of King Herod the Great. He did not have much power because of the Roman rulers who had taken over.

Jeers or Cheers?

Why did the crowds change their cheers for Jesus into jeers? On Sunday people had greeted Jesus with shouts of praise. On Friday morning, crowds demanded his death.

Most people in Jerusalem didn't even know about Jesus' arrest. When they woke up after six o'clock Friday morning, Jesus had already been condemned to death.

The "Crucify him!" crowd probably was a different group of people from the Palm Sunday crowd. They may have been the people who worked at the Temple. This priest-controlled Temple staff—which numbered well over ten thousand people—had probably been persuaded by the priests to condemn Jesus to death.

17

Friday Morning after Six O'clock: Crucify Him!

Matthew 27:15–26; Mark 15:6–15; Luke 23:13–25; John 18:38–19:16

At dawn an angry crowd gathered at the Roman judgment hall. Pilate tried to quiet them.

"Neither Herod nor I find this man guilty," explained Pilate. "We don't think Jesus has done anything to deserve death. But you have a custom that I should set free one Jewish prisoner at the Passover. So on this Passover Feast I will have Jesus whipped. Then I will let him go."

The people shouted back, "No! No! Kill him!"

"But whom should I set free for Passover?" Pilate asked the noisy crowd.

The people cried out, "Set Barabbas free!"

(Barabbas was in prison for murder, robbery, and causing riots. He had caused a lot of trouble, but the priests persuaded the people to ask for his release.)

Pilate still wanted to set Jesus free. So he asked the crowd once again, "Then what should I do with Jesus?"

"Crucify him!" shouted the crowd.

"Why should he die?" Pilate asked the angry mob. "What wrong has he done?"

The people only shouted louder, "Crucify him! Away with him. Crucify him!"

Pilate wiped his forehead as he sent Jesus to be whipped. A little later he brought Jesus out and said to the crowd, "Here is Jesus. I find him innocent."

The Jews said, "But our law says that he must die. He claimed to be the Son of God."

Pilate tried to reason with the crowd.

But the people shouted and stamped their feet.

"If you let this man go," they warned Pilate, "you are not Caesar's friend! Anyone who claims to be a king is against Caesar!"

By now it was just after six in the morning. Pilate sat down in his judgment seat. He pointed to Jesus and told the people, "Here is your king."

The crowd chanted loudly, "Crucify him! Crucify him!"

"Shall I crucify your king?" Pilate asked.

They answered, "He is not our king! We have no king but Caesar of Rome! Crucify him!"

Sweat ran down Pilate's face. He looked around at the angry faces and clenched fists. His heart pounded as he tried to decide what to do with Jesus.

Why didn't Pilate want to sentence Jesus to death?

Why do you think the people wanted Jesus to be crucified?

When have you given in to pressure and done what others wanted?

"Jesus said, 'If you want to follow me, you must say no to yourself. You must take your cross every day and follow me'" (Luke 9:23).

Cat-of-Nine-Tails

Roman whippings nearly killed their victims. First a person was stripped of his clothes. Then his arms were tied to a flogging post. Finally two soldiers took turns beating him with their whips.

The whip that was probably used on Jesus was known as the cat-of-nine-tails. It had nine leather cords attached to a wooden handle. Small, sharp objects—hard lead balls, scraps of metal, and broken pieces of sheep bones—were tied into the cords.

Every stroke of the whip ripped open the skin of the victim's back. This whipping caused a lot of bleeding. The Jews ruled that only thirty-nine lashes could be given at a time to any person. But the Romans had no limitations.

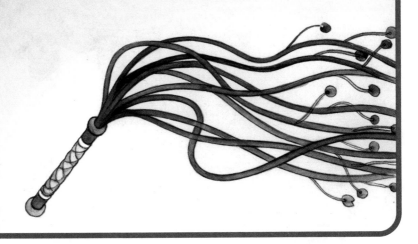

Roman Soldiers

Roman soldiers were trained to torture and kill people. They used any amount of force necessary against those who rebelled against the Roman rule. They tortured people right up to the point of death but without killing them.

Roman soldiers were well known for their cruelty. It has been written that they even threw jars of live poisonous snakes into their enemies' ships!

Every Roman soldier carried three main weapons: a dagger, a three-foot sword, and a six-foot-long spear that could be thrown like a javelin.

Soldiers also carried wooden shields covered with leather and decorated with metal.

18

Mocking the King

Matthew 27:24–31; Mark 15:16–20; John 19:1–3

Pilate knew the crowd was upset and angry. He feared they would start a fight. Because Pilate didn't want any trouble, he decided to give the crowd what they wanted— he would sentence Jesus to be crucified on the cross.

First Pilate asked for a bowl of water. Then he washed his hands in front of the crowd.

"I am not guilty of this man's death," he said. "I wash my hands of his blood. All of you are guilty of his death!"

So Pilate gave orders to the guards to free the prisoner named Barabbas. And he handed Jesus over to the Roman soldiers to be crucified.

The soldiers took Jesus away. The whole company of soldiers was called together in the courtyard.

They had heard Pilate call Jesus "the king of the Jews," so the soldiers came to make fun of Jesus. Taking off his outer clothes, they dressed him up in a purple robe.

The soldiers laughed at Jesus and made fun of him. None of them thought he was a real king. He looked too weak and helpless.

Some of the soldiers cut some long branches from a nearby thornbush. They wove them together in a large circle to make a thorny crown. Then they shoved the thorny crown on Jesus' head.

One soldier put a stick in Jesus' right hand.

"Here's your crown and scepter, O mighty king!" said the soldier. Everyone laughed at how Jesus looked.

All of this time, Jesus never said a word.

Mocking him, the men fell on their knees, pretending to honor him. Then some of the soldiers spit on Jesus. They ridiculed him and said, "Hail, king of the Jews! We honor you!"

One of the men grabbed the stick out of Jesus' hand and beat him over the head with it. The crown of thorns cut deeply in Jesus' forehead and scalp.

Blood ran down Jesus' face. He took the pain without fighting back. And he patiently endured all of the mean treatment. The soldiers probably wondered why he didn't curse them or fight back.

Finally the soldiers got tired of poking fun at Jesus. They took off the purple robe and put his own clothes back on him. Then they led him away to be crucified.

Why didn't Jesus fight back when the soldiers mistreated him? Why was Jesus willing to suffer? How does it make you feel to know Jesus suffered for all that you have done wrong?

The LORD said, "My servant was arrested and sentenced to death. . . . He was cut off from this life. He was punished for the sins of my people" (Isaiah 53:8).

The Silent Lamb

All through the unfair trials and the harsh treatment, Jesus remained silent. Long ago the prophet Isaiah had written this would happen to "the servant of the LORD":

"The LORD says . . . 'My servant suffered the things we should have suffered. He took on himself the pain that should have been ours. . . . His wounds have healed us. . . . He was beaten down and made to suffer. But he didn't open his mouth. He was led away like a sheep to be killed. Lambs are silent while their wool is being cut off. In the same way, he didn't open his mouth'" (Isaiah 52:13; 53:4, 5, 7).

When Jesus suffered on this day, nobody—not even the disciples—understood that he was God's own perfect Lamb, who willingly gave up his life for the world.

Death by Crucifixion

During a short period of time in history, crucifixion was used as the main form of execution. Hanging on a cross was a slow and painful death. Some people hung there for as long as nine days before they died.

Roman citizens could not be crucified. Slaves, pirates, and political or religious rebels were crucified.

Crucifixions were held near public places like main roads and highways. The Romans wanted the local people to see what would happen if they rebelled. The crime of each criminal was written on a board which was nailed on the top of the cross or hung around the criminal's neck.

Death by crucifixion was one of the cruelest forms of punishment ever practiced. Crucifixion was finally forbidden some years after Jesus' death.

19

Early Friday Morning: Carry the Cross

Matthew 27:32; Mark 15:21; Luke 23:26–32; John 19:17

All Thursday night and also early Friday morning, Jesus had been mistreated.

He was taken from the garden to the high priest's house, then to Pilate, then to Herod, and then returned to Pilate. He probably was not given any food to eat or water to drink during this time.

Finally, after the soldiers had whipped Jesus and made fun of him, they tied a heavy wooden crossbeam to the back of his shoulders and arms.

Prisoners condemned to die on a cross usually carried their own crossbeam to the place of crucifixion. The beam weighed between thirty and fifty pounds.

The main pole of the cross was already in place on the top of the hill called Golgotha.

The soldiers forced Jesus to carry his own crossbeam through the narrow city streets and out the city gate to the place of execution on the hill.

Two other men were also led out of the city of Jerusalem to be crucified along with Jesus. They were both robbers.

As Jesus struggled to carry his load, he stumbled and then fell down. He was too weak to get back up with the heavy beam tied across his shoulders.

The soldiers knew Jesus did not have the strength to carry his load any further. They untied the heavy beam from his arms. Since they didn't want to carry it, they looked around for someone else to do the work.

A man named Simon was standing beside the street when Jesus fell. Simon had come to Jerusalem to celebrate Passover. His home was in the city of Cyrene in Africa.

The soldiers grabbed Simon and ordered him to help Jesus. They tied Jesus' crossbeam across Simon's back. He carried it the rest of the way to Golgotha.

By now many Passover visitors were awake and out in the streets. News traveled quickly as they found out what had happened to Jesus during the night. A great crowd gathered as the people followed Jesus through the streets.

Some women wept loudly when they saw Jesus. They couldn't believe this was happening to him.

Jesus turned to the women and said, "Daughters of Jerusalem, do not cry for me. Times of great sorrow and trouble lie ahead for this city. Cry for yourselves and for your children."

Why was crucifixion such a cruel punishment?
Why would God allow his own Son to be crucified?
What do you think Simon felt like when he carried the crossbeam for Jesus? How do you think you might have felt?

"The LORD's servant was killed even though he hadn't harmed anyone. And he had never lied to anyone" (Isaiah 53:9).

Simon of Cyrene

We don't know much about Simon, the man who was forced to carry Jesus' crossbeam to the place of execution. We are told by Matthew that he was from the city of Cyrene in northern Africa (Matthew 27:32). He could have been a black man, but that is not certain.

The gospel of Mark says that the soldiers led Jesus through the city streets at the same time Simon was coming into Jerusalem from the country. He may have been a rich landowner or a common worker in the fields. Perhaps he looked strong and healthy from outdoor work. That may have been one reason why the soldiers picked him.

Mark also writes that Simon "was the father of Alexander and Rufus." These two sons of Simon must have been well known among believers at that time (Mark 15:21).

Golgotha

The hill called Golgotha is at the north end of Mount Moriah. Here God gave his Son as a sacrifice for us.

This is also the same mountain where God had asked Abraham to sacrifice his son, Isaac. After Abraham built an altar, he prepared to sacrifice his son to God. But God stopped him and gave him a ram (a male sheep) to be sacrificed in the place of Isaac (Genesis 22:1–19).

There is a hill outside the walls of Jerusalem where you can see a "skull." When the sun shines, the rocks form shadows of two eyes, a nose, and a mouth. People think this may be the hill where Jesus was crucified.

Golgotha means "The Place of the Skull." The hill may also have been named this because so many people died there.

20

Nine O'clock: Nailed to the Cross

Matthew 27:33–38; Mark 15:22–27; Luke 23:33–38; John 19:17–24

The Roman soldiers led Jesus to the hill called Golgotha. Then they offered Jesus some vinegar wine mixed with spices. This drink would have helped take away some of the pain of the crucifixion.

But Jesus would not drink the vinegar wine. He was willing to endure all the pain and all the suffering as he gave his life for us.

It was nine o'clock in the morning when the Roman soldiers crucified Jesus. First they laid him down on the wooden cross. They hammered the nails through his wrists and then tied his arms to the crossbeam with ropes. His feet were nailed to a small block of wood near the bottom of the cross.

Instead of cursing the soldiers, Jesus said a prayer for them. "Father, forgive them," he prayed. "They don't know what they are doing."

Pilate ordered the charge against Jesus to be written on a board and nailed above the cross. The sign said, "This is Jesus of Nazareth, King of the Jews." The words were written in the three main languages—Greek, Hebrew, and Latin—so all who went in and out of the city could read it.

The two thieves were also crucified with Jesus. One man was placed on the right side of Jesus' cross. The other was crucified on his left.

When Jesus was crucified between the two thieves, this made the Scripture come true which said, "The LORD's servant was willing to give his life as a sacrifice. He was counted among those who had committed crimes" (Isaiah 53:12).

After the soldiers nailed Jesus to the cross, they divided his clothes, one piece for each of them. But they saw that his outer robe was made from a single piece of cloth. It had been woven from top to bottom without a seam.

So the soldiers said to each other, "Let's not tear this robe. We can cast lots and gamble to see who gets it."

Then the words of Psalm 22:18 came true: "They divide up my clothes among them. They cast lots for what I am wearing."

Afterward the soldiers sat down on some nearby rocks and waited for Jesus and the two thieves to die.

Why do you think the soldiers gambled for Jesus' clothes?
Are you grateful that Jesus was willing to suffer and die on the cross?
How do you feel when you read about the things Jesus suffered?

"We have been set free because of what Christ has done. Through his blood our sins have been forgiven" (Ephesians 1:7).

Casting Lots for Clothes

The average person of Jesus' time usually wore four pieces of clothing: an inner tunic, an outer robe, a belt, and some leather sandals.

The soldiers on guard duty at the cross took off Jesus' clothes before they crucified him. They divided up the clothing by casting lots. This was a lot like throwing dice.

People would cast lots by putting different colored stones in a jar and shaking the jar until one stone jumped out. There were other ways to gamble using sticks.

Jesus had a fine cloak which was made of one piece of cloth. To divide it and tear it apart would have ruined it. So the soldiers at the cross cast lots to see who would get it. When they gambled for Jesus' clothes, the Scripture prophecy came true (Psalm 22:18).

Blood Pays for Sin

Once each year the high priest went into the third inner room of the Temple. This back room was called the "Most Holy Place." Jewish people thought of this as God's home on earth. The priest carried the blood of an animal sacrifice with him. He sprinkled the blood on the ark of the covenant as he prayed for God to forgive everyone's sin.

God is a holy and perfect God. But people are not perfect. Sin is a serious problem with no simple way to get rid of it.

God set up sacrifices as a means of forgiveness. God told Moses, "The life of the creature is in its blood. . . . Blood is life. That is why blood pays for your sin" (Leviticus 16:34).

When Jesus died, he took our sin once for all (1 Peter 3:18). He made a trade with us. He took our sin and suffered its punishment. He gives us his goodness and makes us right with God. Now God sees us as holy and spotless. And animals don't have to die in our place anymore.

21

Late Friday Morning: Scorned and Mocked

Matthew 27:39–44; Mark 15:29–32; Luke 23:35–43

The Roman soldiers crucified Jesus and the two thieves beside a busy road where thousands of Passover visitors traveled in and out of the city of Jerusalem.

When some of the people passed by the crosses, they shouted at Jesus and made fun of him. They shook their heads and mocked him, saying, "You said you could destroy the Temple and build it again in three days. Let's see you save yourself. If you are the Son of God, then come down from the cross!"

Many priests and the Pharisees also came out to the hill and made fun of Jesus. They stood together at the roadside and jeered.

"He saved others," said the Pharisees. "Now he can't save himself! Let this Christ—this king of Israel—come down from the cross! When we see him do that, we will believe. He trusts in God, so let God rescue him now—if he wants him. For he told us, 'I am the Son of God.'"

The soldiers also came up and poked fun at Jesus. They shoved a sponge with wine vinegar in his face. But he wouldn't drink it.

And they laughed at Jesus, saying, "If you are the king of the Jews, why don't you save yourself?"

One of the thieves hanging there also made fun of Jesus. He cried out, "Aren't you the Christ? Then save yourself! And save us too!"

The second thief scolded the first thief. "Don't you have any respect for God?" he asked. "Remember, you are under the same sentence of death as Jesus is. We are being punished fairly. We are getting everything we deserve. But Jesus hasn't done anything wrong."

Then he turned to Jesus with one last prayer. He said, "Remember me when you come into your kingdom."

Jesus slowly turned his head to the thief and gave him a wonderful promise. "What I'm about to tell you is true," said Jesus. "Today you will be with me in paradise."

That thief was one of the few people who still believed in Jesus as the promised Messiah sent from God.

To those who watched Jesus hanging helplessly on the cross, it looked as if he were totally defeated. People lost all hope that he was their Savior and Messiah.

Could Jesus have come down from the cross? Why didn't he?
Do you think the priests would have believed in Jesus if he had come down from the cross? Why or why not?
Why should you take time to thank Jesus for all he has done?

"When the name of Jesus is spoken, everyone's knee will bow to worship him" (Philippians 2:10).

Every Knee Will Bow

Jesus looked defeated when he died, but he had actually won the victory over sin, death, and hell. Someday everyone will kneel before Jesus, the victorious King.

The apostle Paul explains this: "Jesus made himself nothing. He took on the very nature of a servant. He was made in human form. He appeared as a human being. He came down to the lowest level. He obeyed God completely, even though it led to his death. In fact, he died on a cross.

"So God lifted him up to the highest place. He gave him the name that is above every name. When the name of Jesus is spoken, everyone's knee will bow to worship him. . . . Everyone's mouth will say that Jesus Christ is Lord" (Philippians 2:7–11).

Have *you* bowed your knees to Jesus? Is he your Lord?

John

John and his older brother James were fishermen at the Sea of Galilee with their father Zebedee. John's mother may have been Salome, a sister of Mary. If Salome was his mother, then John was one of Jesus' cousins.

John was the youngest of the twelve disciples. And we know that he also was one of Jesus' closest friends.

He called himself the disciple "whom Jesus loved" (John 13:23; 19:26; 20:2; 21:7, 20). He was with Jesus during many special times—when Jesus raised a girl from the dead (Luke 8:51), was transfigured (Luke 9:28–29), and prayed in the garden (Matthew 26:37).

Later John wrote the gospel of John and three letters (epistles). And when he was old, God showed him the visions of the book of Revelation.

22

Friday Noon:
Darkness Falls

Matthew 27:45–49; Mark 15:33–36; Luke 23:44–49; John 19:25–30

It seems that John, one of Jesus' disciples, was the only disciple who stood near the cross of Jesus and watched everything that happened.

Some women also stood beside John. Mary, the mother of Jesus, was there. So were Salome, the sister of Mary, along with Mary Magdalene and Mary, the wife of Cleopas.

Tears ran down John's face. It hurt him to see how much Jesus was suffering. He loved Jesus. And he knew Jesus loved him.

Then John saw Jesus look over at him and then at Mary, Jesus' mother.

Showing his love for Mary in a special way, Jesus said to her, "Dear woman, here is your son." And he told John, "Here is your mother."

John knew he was supposed to take care of Mary. And from that hour he took Mary into his home and treated her like his own mother.

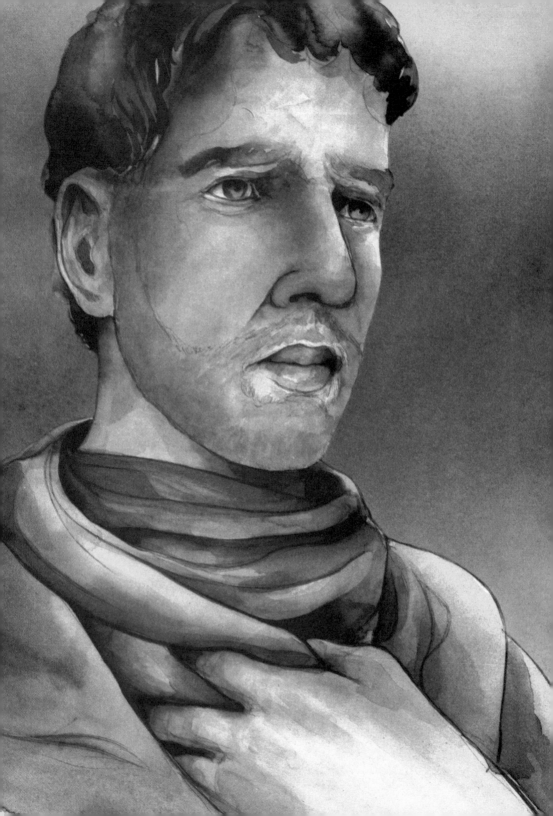

At twelve o'clock noon, the sky overhead grew black. The earth was covered with heavy darkness that lasted until three o'clock in the afternoon.

John saw the soldiers look nervously at the sky. Everyone wondered what was happening.

The crowds standing around the cross grew quiet. Even the Pharisees and the soldiers stopped talking. They all stood silently in the darkness.

About three o'clock, Jesus cried out in a loud voice. He said, "My God, my God, why have you deserted me?"

John wondered what Jesus meant. *Did God really leave Jesus? And why did Jesus say, 'My God'? Why didn't he call to God and say, 'My Father'?*

Other people who were standing near the cross also wondered at what Jesus said.

They told each other, "Listen, this man is calling for Elijah the prophet. Leave him alone. Let's see if Elijah will come to save him from the cross."

On that special afternoon no one knew that this death was the most important event that had ever happened in the history of the world.

Jesus' death on the cross was opening a door into heaven—a way for all of us to come to God and to know God. It was his best gift.

Why did God leave Jesus all alone on the cross for a moment? Do you think there was any other way for Jesus to save us? Why not? What would you have thought or done if you had been standing near the cross that day?

"Without the spilling of blood, no one can be forgiven" (Hebrews 9:22).

Kinds of Crosses

Several different kinds of crosses were used for the execution of criminals. The Bible states that a sign was placed above Jesus' head. So Jesus was most likely crucified on a cross shaped like a "t."

This was the moment for which Jesus had been born. He was sent from heaven to take all of the punishment we deserve. He was sent to die in our place.

His name—Jesus—means "Savior." His death on the cross is what makes him a Savior.

Remember what an angel of the Lord told Joseph in a dream: "Don't be afraid to take Mary home as your wife. The baby inside her is from the Holy Spirit. She is going to have a son. You must give him the name Jesus. That is because he will save his people from their sins" (Matthew 1:20–21).

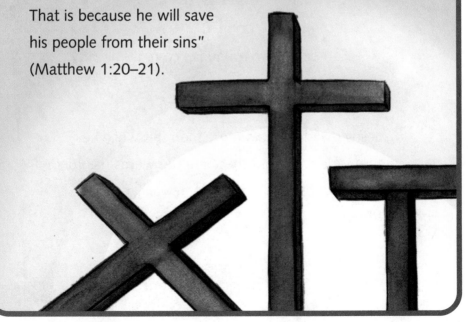

Last Words of Jesus

1. "Father, forgive them. They don't know what they are doing" (Luke 23:34).

2. "Today you will be with me in paradise" (Luke 23:43).

3. Jesus said to Mary, his mother, "Dear woman, here is your son."
   And Jesus said to John, his disciple, "Here is your mother" (John 19:26).

4. "My God, my God, why have you deserted me?" (Matthew 27:46).

5. "I am thirsty" (John 19:28).

6. "It is finished" (John 19:30).

7. "Father, into your hands I commit my very life" (Luke 23:46).

Jesus may have said more than this while he hung on the cross, but these are the words recorded by the four gospel writers: Matthew, Mark, Luke, and John.

23

Friday—Three O'clock: Final Moments

Luke 23:46; John 29:28–35

Jesus had refused the drink offered to him before he was nailed to the cross. The sour wine vinegar was offered to every man who was to be crucified. Jesus knew it would have dulled some of the pain.

But now Jesus knew that everything was finished. His work was done. He had been hanging on the cross for six hours. He could barely speak because his mouth was so dry. There was something more Jesus needed to say—something very important—before he died.

So Jesus asked for a drink, saying, "I am thirsty."

When the soldiers heard what Jesus said, they came to help him.

A jar of wine vinegar had been placed on the ground close to the cross. One of the soldiers soaked a sponge in the jar. He put the sponge on the long stem of a hyssop plant and lifted it up to Jesus' lips so he could drink from it.

By now it was almost three o'clock in the afternoon. The earth had been covered in darkness for three hours.

Jesus drank the vinegar to get his throat wet enough so he could speak. Then he shouted out in a loud voice, "It is FINISHED!" And everyone heard him.

Jesus had completed his work. It was all done. Now Jesus cried out once more to God and said, "Father, into your hands I commit my very life."

Then Jesus breathed his last breath—and he died.

At this time only a few hours were left before the special Passover Sabbath began at six o'clock that evening. The priests didn't want any dying bodies left hanging on the cross, since the next day was a day of celebration.

So they went to Pilate and asked if the victims' legs could be broken. Breaking their legs would make them die faster because they could no longer raise themselves up to breathe. Once they had died, their bodies could be taken down from the cross before the Sabbath began.

The soldiers broke the legs of the thieves, speeding up their deaths. But when they came to Jesus, he had already died. Just to make sure he was dead, one soldier shoved a spear in his side. When blood and water ran out, the soldier did not break his legs. He knew Jesus had died.

What were some words Jesus said on the cross?

What do you think Jesus meant when he said, "It is finished"?

Why is it important to remember what Jesus did, even when it hurts us to do so?

"The LORD watches over all of their bones. Not one of them will be broken" (Psalm 34:20).

Did Jesus Really Die?

What happened when the Roman soldier stuck his spear into Jesus' side? It went under the bottom rib and cut into the sac of fluid around the heart of Jesus.

This soldier was not trying to kill Jesus. He knew that blood and water flowing from the wound proved Jesus had already died. Everyone's blood separates at death. If Jesus had been alive, only blood would have spurted out with every beat of his heart.

John saw this happen and he wrote it down. Now the Scripture came true: "Not one of his bones will be broken" (Exodus 12:46; Numbers 9:12; Psalm 34:20).
Also: "They will look to . . . the one they have pierced" (Zechariah 12:10).

Blow the Shofar!

At three o'clock every afternoon, a loud horn sounded from the Temple. It was the noise of the "shofar"—the great ram's horn.

A shofar is made from the long, curved horn of a ram (an adult male sheep). Shofars come in all different sizes, shapes, and lengths. Some horns are short—about a foot long. Others can be two to three feet long.

Much practice is needed to blow a shofar. The Temple priest had to take a deep breath. He needed to blow a long and loud blast instead of a short blast.

This horn was blown to announce the sacrifice of a lamb which always happened at exactly three o'clock each afternoon in the Temple.

24

At Three O'clock: Amazing Happenings

Matthew 27:50–56; Mark 15:37–41; Luke 23:44–49; John 19:30

At exactly three o'clock on Friday, Jesus cried out, "It is FINISHED!" But Jesus did not mean, "My life is over." He meant, "It is done! I did it!" He had finished the work he came to do—to give his life as the Lamb of God.

Just before Jesus died, a priest had climbed up to the corner wall of the Temple court, just as he did every afternoon. At exactly three o'clock, he lifted a ram's horn to his mouth and blew it hard and long.

In the court below, the priest slit the throat of a lamb. Another priest caught the lamb's blood in a bowl and offered it on the altar for the daily midafternoon sacrifice.

This sacrifice had taken place every day at three o'clock for more than twelve hundred years!

When the people of the city heard the sound of the shofar, they stopped what they were doing. They silently thought about the lamb being offered to God. And they thanked God for receiving the blood of the lamb as a sacrifice for all their failures and their wrongdoing.

Also at this same time, the thick curtain in the Temple ripped right down the center, from the top to the bottom!

This curtain was hanging in front of the special entrance into the Most Holy Place, the room at the back of the Temple.

An earthquake also struck at this time. The ground shook. Large rocks split apart. People ran in all directions.

In the cemeteries outside the city gates, some graves broke open and the bodies of many of God's people who had died were raised to life.

The Roman officer in charge of the crucifixion was standing near the cross. He had watched Jesus during the long hours that he hung on the cross. He had heard what Jesus said. He had seen how Jesus died.

When the earthquake struck, the officer and all the soldiers with him shook with fear. They did not understand what was happening. And the officer cried out, "This man was really the Son of God!"

After Jesus died, the heavy darkness lifted and the sun peeked out from behind the clouds.

Now that Jesus was dead, many people left who had been watching the crucifixion. They felt very sad as they went back to their homes. Their dreams and hopes of a Messiah had died with Jesus.

Some of the women who had followed Jesus to Jerusalem watched from a distance. These women had helped Jesus when he was teaching and healing people in Galilee. Now they hugged each other and cried.

Name some of the events that happened when Jesus died.

What did a Roman officer say about Jesus? Why did he say it?

How do you think Jesus' followers felt as they watched him die?

"Jesus our priest offered one sacrifice for sins for all time"
(Hebrews 10:1).

The Temple Curtain

God's presence filled the Most Holy Place inside the Temple. No one except the high priest was allowed in this room. If anyone else entered the room, they died. Even the high priest could not enter without the blood of an animal.

The doorway to the room was covered with a heavy curtain fifteen feet high—twice as high as ceilings in most homes. The curtain was thick and very heavy. It took many men to lift it. Pictures of angels were woven into its design made out of blue, purple, and red yarns and linen cloth.

The curtain tore apart when Jesus died. It could never have ripped by itself, especially from top to bottom. And no person could have torn the whole thing in half. This was a signal from God. Jesus died so we could have peace with God. We can go to God in prayer. Now we can ask God's forgiveness. And we can worship God without fear.

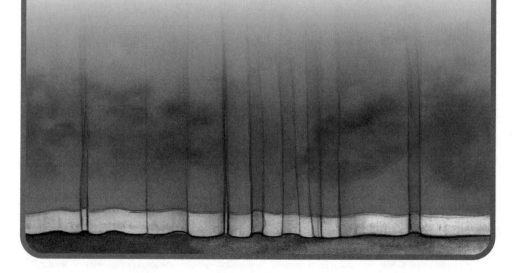

Joseph—A Fearless Follower

Joseph was a rich man from the city of Arimathea who loved God. He was a leading member of the Jewish council, but he also was a secret follower of Jesus (Matthew 27:57). Joseph had just finished carving a tomb for himself and his family in a rocky hillside. It had taken a lot of work and a lot of money. Large family tombs often cost as much as a house! Only rich people could afford them. Most Jewish people were buried in the ground, not in tombs.

This new tomb was still empty. It had never held a dead body. That was important because Jewish law said that only people who were related could be buried in the same tomb.

When Joseph gave Jesus his tomb, it was an expensive gift! Now Joseph could never be buried in it. Neither could anyone else in his family.

25

Friday Afternoon: Special Gifts for Jesus

Matthew 27:57–61; Mark 15:42–47; Luke 23:50–56; John 19:38–42

The Romans did not care how long people hung on the cross after they died. Sometimes they let victims hang there for days. But Jewish laws stated that people had to be buried on the day of their execution.

So when Joseph of Arimathea knew Jesus had died, he went to Pilate and asked permission to take the body of Jesus down from the cross and bury him.

Joseph had secretly followed Jesus because he feared his fellow Jewish leaders. He had not agreed with their arrest and trial of Jesus. Joseph knew he could get in trouble if he helped bury Jesus. The priests could have him banned from the Temple.

Pilate didn't believe Jesus was already dead. He sent for the soldier in charge of the crucifixion and asked him for a report.

The soldier explained that Jesus had died quickly— in only six hours. When Pilate was sure Jesus was dead, he gave Joseph permission to bury his body.

Jewish customs required that two or more people would prepare a body for burial.

So Nicodemus, another secret follower of Jesus, came to help bury Jesus. He brought seventy-five pounds of spices and aloes to put on Jesus' body.

Joseph bought some new linen cloth in which to wrap the body. He had decided to bury Jesus in his own new tomb in a nearby garden.

Nicodemus and Joseph carefully lowered Jesus' body down from the cross and carried it to the garden.

The burial of Jesus had to be done quickly. Only a few hours were left before the Saturday Sabbath began.

The Jewish Sabbath day began at sunset—around six—on Friday evening. Work on the Sabbath day was forbidden. It was to be a day of rest and prayer.

After washing Jesus' body, the two men wrapped it in one long piece of cloth. They spread spices and aloe on smaller strips of cloth that were then wrapped around the body of Jesus.

They laid Jesus' body on a stone shelf with a stone "pillow" under his head. Then they went outside and rolled an extremely large stone in front of the door.

Some women stood close by, watching Joseph and Nicodemus. They saw how the body of Jesus had been buried. They also wanted to show their love for Jesus. But since it was almost sundown, they had to return home to rest on the Sabbath.

Why did Joseph ask Pilate for the body of Jesus?

Did anyone believe Jesus would rise from the dead? Who?

Would it have been easy to take Jesus' body OUT of the grave wrappings? Why or why not?

"Christ's death has made you holy in God's sight. So now you don't have any flaw. You are free from blame" (Colossians 1:22).

Preparing the Body

More is known about the burial of Jesus than is known about the burial of any person in all of ancient history.

After washing the body of Jesus, Joseph and Nicodemus clothed him in handmade white garments made from plain cloth. A long piece of linen cloth was laid from the back of Jesus' neck down to his feet. They pulled the cloth over his feet and up to the top of his chest.

The men mixed the myrrh, aloe, and spices and smeared the sticky mass on the body and the cloths.

Smaller strips of cloth were tightly wound around the body. These strips held the spices close to the body.

When the gummy spices harden, it is very difficult to unwrap the cloths.

Finally a smaller piece of cloth was wrapped around Jesus' head. This was called the "facecloth."

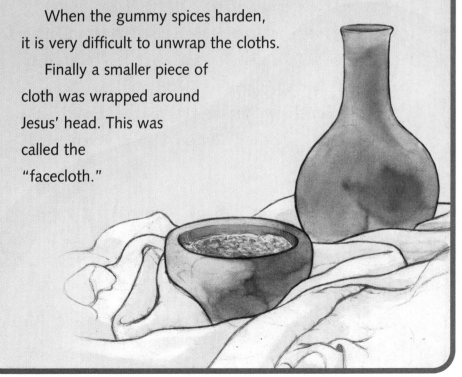

The Great Seal of Rome

The Roman seal placed around Jesus' grave was like the yellow tape that police use at a crime scene. It "sealed off" an area to prevent robbery or vandalism.

Once King Darius used his signet ring and the signet rings of his nobles to seal the lions' den when Daniel was inside (Daniel 6:17).

Roman soldiers strung a cord across the rock in front of Jesus' tomb. They used soft clay or melted wax to "glue" the cord on the hillside on both sides of the rock.

A "signet ring" with the official seal of the Roman governor was pressed into the clay before it hardened.

This seal made it easy to tell if the stone had been moved. Any movement would have pulled the cords out of the clay, breaking the seal. The seal was also a reminder of the powerful Roman Empire's protection of Jesus' body.

The punishment for breaking (or even scratching) a Roman seal was instant death!

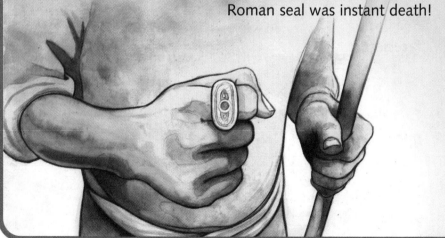

26

All Day Saturday: Guards in Place

Matthew 27:62–66

After the body of Jesus was taken down from the cross, the priests and the Pharisees felt relieved. Finally Jesus was dead. His miracle works had been stopped. The Jewish leaders hoped that his followers would leave Jerusalem and return to their own towns around the Sea of Galilee.

Yet now that Jesus had been buried, the priests and Pharisees also knew they might have a bigger problem.

They wondered what would happen if the disciples of Jesus told people that Jesus was alive? Would the disciples dare to open the tomb and steal his body? Would they try to fool the crowds by making up a story that Jesus had risen from the dead?

The priests and Pharisees knew they had to keep Jesus' body from being stolen. So early on Saturday morning, they went back to the Roman governor's house with another request.

"Sir," the Pharisees said to Pilate, "we remember something that liar Jesus said while he was still alive. He told people, 'After three days I will rise again.'

"So we want you to give the order to guard the tomb of Jesus until the third day. If you don't do this, his disciples might come and steal the body. Then they will lie and say that Jesus has come alive. This last lie will be worse than the first lie—that he was the Messiah."

Pilate didn't argue with the Jewish leaders. He let them have their way.

"Take some soldiers," Pilate said to them. "Do the best you can to guard the tomb."

The priests and Pharisees left Pilate's house. They took a guard unit to the hillside where they knew Jesus was buried. They stretched a long cord across the stone that covered the grave's entrance. After fastening the cord with clay at both sides of the stone, they stamped the seal of the Roman Empire in the clay. Then the guard unit was placed on twenty-four-hour duty in front of the tomb.

Now the Jewish leaders felt satisfied. No one could get past these powerful, armed guards who stood in front of the tomb. No one would dare to break the Roman seal and risk being put to death.

The leaders were sure that none of the disciples of Jesus would ever be able to steal the body of Jesus now. Finally they were rid of him . . . or so they thought.

Why did the Jewish leaders insist that the tomb had to be guarded? Do you think the disciples would try to steal Jesus' body? Why not? Why is it important to know that Jesus died and didn't just faint?

"Christ's body was put to death. But the Holy Spirit brought him back to life" (1 Peter 3:18).

Roman Guards

Roman guard units numbered from four to sixteen soldiers. They were an awesome fighting group. Each man was trained to protect six feet of ground.

Four men were placed directly in front of what they were to guard. The other men would rest or sleep in a semicircle in front of them. Four men kept watch during a four-hour shift. One unit of men always had to be alert and on duty.

It would have been impossible for a thief to get past ONE guard, let alone SIXTEEN guards, even if they were asleep. No one could have moved the stone, taken Jesus' body out of the cloths, and left without being seen.

The Great Stone

After Jesus was wrapped in cloths and spices weighing over one hundred pounds, his body was sealed behind a stone that weighed between two thousand and four thousand pounds. His disciples never thought they would see him again.

A hillside grave was usually closed with a huge stone. It protected the grave from thieves and wild animals.

One large stone usually took only a couple men to push it down the channel of about twelve to eighteen inches wide. This channel was dug alongside the base of the hill. It slanted downhill to the front of the tomb. Once the stone was pushed down over the opening, it could take as many as twenty men to push it back up the channel, away from the entrance.

27

Early Sunday Morning: Surprise!

Matthew 28:1–4

Very early Sunday morning, there was a powerful earthquake. It shook the whole hillside where Jesus was buried.

A brilliant light flashed as a shining angel of the Lord came down from heaven. The angel went to the tomb, rolled back the heavy stone, and sat down on it.

What a sight! The angel's face and body shone like lightning. (Have you ever had lightning strike in front of you?) The angel's clothing was white as snow. (Has sunshine on snow ever blinded you?)

The angel of the Lord did not roll away the stone to let Jesus come out. Jesus had already left the tomb. And he had left his grave clothes behind.

The angel rolled away the stone to let the people in. Now everyone would see that Jesus had done the impossible. He kept his promise—he came alive on the third day!

The Roman soldiers had never guarded a dead body before. Yet they were determined to make sure the Roman seal across the gravestone would not be vandalized or broken.

They weren't worried. The disciples had not tried to rescue Jesus from the cross on Friday. The soldiers knew they wouldn't try to steal him from the grave—they were too scared and helpless.

But the guards were in for a BIG surprise when God's angel suddenly appeared in front of them!

At the sight of the angel, those strong guards were filled with a fear they had never felt before in their lives. Their arms and legs shook violently. The armor on their chests and the helmets on their heads rattled as they shook.

Their arms and legs went limp. None of them were able to pull out their swords. They couldn't attack. Their legs collapsed as they fell in a heap beside the tomb. They became as dead men—unable to move a muscle. All they could do was stare helplessly at the awesome angel.

The powerful guards whom everyone else feared now were overcome by their own fear. For the first time they were totally helpless and overpowered.

All it took was just the sight of God's angel. The angel didn't knock them over, threaten them, or attack them. The angel just showed up! Don't you wish you could have been there and seen it happen?

Was it hard work for the angel to move the stone? Why not?
Why did the angel roll the stone away from the door of the tomb?
How do you think God's angels serve you today?

"God . . . raised Christ from the dead. . . . God placed all things under Christ's rule" (Ephesians 1:20, 22).

What Do Angels Do?

God created angels. These spirit beings are usually never seen. They don't have a body like ours. But sometimes they have been seen in human form.

The word "angel" means "messenger." In the Bible, angels often appeared to bring good news from God.

The first person mentioned in the Bible who saw a messenger angel was Hagar. The angel told her to go back to Abraham and Sarah, and she obeyed (Genesis 16:9–15).

Two angels brought God's message to Lot, telling him to leave the city of Sodom (Genesis 19:1–29).

Angels gave directions to Abraham (Genesis 22:11–18), to Elijah (2 Kings 1:1–17), to Philip (Acts 8:26–40), and to Cornelius, a Roman captain (Acts 10:1–33).

But the best message ever brought by an angel was the message *"HE IS RISEN!"*

When Guards Fail

Roman soldiers took great care to complete and finish all their assigned duties. They knew they would receive harsh punishment if they failed. The penalty of death was given to any guard who left his night watch.

If a guard was caught sleeping, sitting down, or even leaning against something while on duty, his clothes would be set on fire—while he was still wearing them!

The soldiers at Jesus' tomb had completely failed in their duties. The Roman seal had been broken. The grave had been opened. And the body of Jesus was missing.

According to Roman law, the whole guard unit should have been immediately executed!

28

Big Trouble for the Guards

Matthew 28:11–15

The guards finally got up off the ground. They did not know how to explain what they had seen. Who was the powerful bright being? Where had he gone?

And who had rolled back the heavy gravestone? How could it have been moved so far away from the grave? It wasn't even in the channel where it should be.

Looking inside the tomb, the soldiers saw the grave clothes still wrapped up and lying on the stone slab. But the body the soldiers were supposed to be guarding was gone. The burial wrappings were empty!

How could someone steal the body of Jesus without unwrapping the tightly wound grave clothes?

The guards knew they were in terrible trouble. Perhaps they talked about what they should do. They knew it wouldn't work to try to run away. They would only be hunted down, caught sooner or later, and then killed for their failure to keep the seal from being broken and Jesus' body from being stolen.

There was no reason to stay and guard an empty tomb. So the guards did the only thing they could do— they decided to tell the truth to the Temple priests.

But now the guards had a new worry. Could they find anyone who would believe their story?

When they arrived at the Temple, the guards asked to see the priests. And the guards told them everything that had happened that morning at the tomb.

The priests were very upset when they heard the soldiers' report. After talking over the problem, the priests came up with a special plan.

First they gave the soldiers a large amount of money.

Next they instructed the soldiers, "You must tell the people: 'Jesus' disciples came to the grave during the night. They stole his body while we were sleeping.'"

The Jewish leaders promised to keep the guards out of trouble. They told the guards, "If the governor hears this report, we will pay him off. That will keep you from being punished."

So the guards took the money and did as they were told. Even though it would have been impossible for the disciples to steal the body without unwrapping the grave clothes, this story spread among all the people.

What happened to soldiers who failed in their duties?

What was wrong with the guards' story? How could they have seen the disciples steal Jesus' body if they were all asleep?

What proofs of the Resurrection help you know Jesus is alive?

"If Christ has not been raised, your faith doesn't mean anything. Your sins have not been forgiven" (1 Corinthians 15:17).

Where's the Body?

All the evidence at the tomb proves that Jesus' body was no longer in the grave:

1. The guards left their post and went to tell the Jewish leaders.
2. The stone was rolled back so everyone could look inside and see that Jesus' body was missing.
3. Mary Magdalene and the other women saw the grave clothes—they were empty!
4. Peter and John also saw the empty grave clothes.
5. No one ever did find Jesus' dead body.
6. Jewish leaders said Jesus' body had been stolen, but they never could prove it.
7. The disciples and many followers did see Jesus, but he was no longer dead— he was ALIVE!

Burial Spices

Jewish people used perfumed spices when they buried their loved ones. The women had seen Nicodemus bring his gift of spices. They also wanted to show their love for Jesus by bringing a gift. Their gift of spices had probably been prepared on Saturday evening after the Sabbath ended.

Burial "spices" were not the same cooking spices we use today. Burial spices were made from pieces of sweet-smelling wood which were ground into powder.

The powder was added to a thick, gooey mixture, such as myrrh, to make a heavy paste. The paste held the grave clothes together and hardened rapidly. The strong spicy smell covered up the smell of death.

The women could have been bringing as much as fifty pounds of spices to the tomb on Sunday morning. But they never got to use their gift—Jesus wasn't dead anymore!

29

Sunday Sunrise: Look Inside!

Matthew 28:1–8; Mark 16:1–8; Luke 24:1–8

The gates of Jerusalem were opened just after sunrise on Sunday morning, the first day of the week. Some of the women, along with Mary Magdalene, Joanna, Salome, and Mary, the mother of James, walked out of the city to the tomb where Jesus had been buried. They brought their gift of burial spices to put on his body.

On their way, the women talked about the stone that covered the opening of the tomb. They asked each other, "Who will roll the stone away from the tomb for us? How will we get inside to use our burial spices?"

The women may not have known about the soldiers who went to guard the tomb on Saturday. These soldiers would have refused to allow the women to go into the sealed tomb.

When the women came within sight of the tomb, they saw the stone—it was rolled away from the entrance. They hurried to the tomb and looked inside. There lay the grave clothes, still wrapped but now empty! Where was Jesus?

Suddenly two men in clothes as bright as lightning stood in front of the women. The women were terrified. They bowed down with their faces to the ground.

One of the angels said to them, "Don't be afraid. I know that you are looking for Jesus, who was crucified. But why do you look for the living among the dead? Jesus is not here! Don't you remember how Jesus told you he would rise? He is alive!"

Speechless, the women could only stare at the bright, shining angel.

The angel said to them, "Remember what Jesus told you. He said, 'The Son of Man must be handed over to his enemies. He must be nailed to a cross. He will die, but on the third day he will rise from the dead.'"

The angel pointed to the burial clothes. "Come and see the place where he lay."

The women slowly moved to the stone slab where the white wrappings lay. They could hardly believe their eyes . . . or their ears!

"Now, go quickly!" said the angel. "Tell his disciples and Peter, 'He has risen from the dead. He is going ahead of you into Galilee. There you will see him.'"

The women ran as fast as they could. Their hearts were full of fear . . . and joy. *Jesus was alive!*

Why did the women go to the tomb early Sunday morning?

What did the angel tell the women?

What does the angel's message mean to you today?

"Christ is the first of those who rise from the dead. When he comes back, those who belong to him will be raised" (1 Corinthians 15:23).

Women Who Followed Jesus

During the time Jesus lived, women were not treated well. Women had no rights. They couldn't own any property. They weren't taught to read or write.

But Jesus treated women with great love and respect. He healed many of them from sickness and evil spirits. These women became followers of Jesus. They helped him and provided meals for him and his disciples.

A group of women stayed near the cross on Friday. They watched while Jesus was buried. They were the first to come to the tomb on Sunday with their gift of spices.

These women had great faith, but they still did not believe they would ever see Jesus alive again. They were coming to the tomb to anoint his dead body.

After Jesus rose from the dead, he appeared to Mary Magdalene and the other women. They all were so happy! They told everyone they met that Jesus was alive!

Inside the Tomb

Come and look inside a tomb like the one in which Jesus was buried. Walk in through the entrance. You might have to bend down, since the doors were usually only four-and-a-half to five feet high.

Right inside the door was a "court," about nine feet square. Here they washed the body and wrapped it for burial. It was also a place where family and friends gathered to mourn their loved one.

In the carved-out cave, benches or platforms were cut out of the stone walls on the sides. These "shelves" of stone were of one piece with the cave walls. The bodies were laid on these slabs.

Later the family would move the stone and reopen the tomb. The bones of their loved one would be placed in a small stone box to make room for other bodies to be buried there.

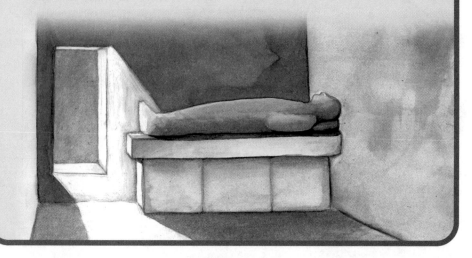

30

Where Is His Body?

Mark 16:9–11; John 20:1–18

Earlier that morning Mary Magdalene sadly carried her basket of spices to the burial grounds outside the city. Carrying the heavy load of spices made her wish that Jewish laws allowed cemeteries inside a city.

Deep in thought, she had walked silently with the other women who were also bringing their gift of burial spices to put on the body of Jesus.

When Mary neared the hillside, she could see the stone moved back from the grave entrance. *Who could have moved it?* she wondered. *Why would anyone want to get inside—oh, they must have stolen Jesus' body!*

Trying to run with her basket, Mary hurried back to the city to find Peter and John. Tears ran down her cheeks as she told them what had happened.

"They have taken the Lord out of the tomb!" she said. "We don't know where they have put his body!"

After hearing the news, Peter and John ran out the door. They raced to the tomb ahead of Mary, who walked down the road for a third time.

The other women had already left the tomb by the time Peter and John came running down the road. The hillside around the grave was deserted. The guards had left long ago.

John ran faster than Peter, so he reached the tomb first. He bent over, but he did not go inside the entrance to the tomb.

As he looked in the low doorway, he could see the linen cloths still lying there. The wrapped cloths were still neatly wound, as if they were wrapped around an invisible body.

Then Peter arrived. He rushed past John into the tomb. There lay the undisturbed grave clothes on the stone slab—but Jesus' body was gone!

Peter felt stunned as he stared at the grave clothes still wound tightly without a body inside. *What happened to Jesus' body?* he wondered. *Who would steal it? Why weren't the grave clothes unwrapped? And how did they take the body without unwrapping the cloths?*

Peter noticed the smaller burial cloth that had been wrapped around Jesus' face. It was lying on the rock, neatly folded but separate from the other wrappings.

Finally John quietly stepped inside the tomb. He touched the wrappings and took a deep breath. "It's true, Peter," he whispered. "Jesus is alive! He has risen!"

Amazed, they stood there a few minutes and stared at the wrappings. Then they hurried back to tell the others.

But at this time neither Peter nor John understood from the Scriptures that Jesus, as the Messiah, needed to die and then rise from the dead.

What did John and Peter do when they arrived at the tomb?

If the body had been stolen, would the cloths have been wrapped?

What would you have thought if you had looked inside the tomb?

"Our Lord Jesus is the great Shepherd of the sheep. The God who gives peace brought him back from the dead" (Hebrews 13:20).

The Burial Facecloth

When Jesus rose from the dead, he didn't need any help getting free from the grave clothes. He just went through them as he went through locked doors. But Jesus took time to neatly fold his linen facecloth and lay it on the stone by itself. This folded cloth had a special meaning to people who lived in the Middle East.

When they went to someone's home for dinner, they would show their happiness or unhappiness with the meal by what they did to their napkin. If they LIKED the dinner and had a good time, then at the end of the meal they would crumple their napkin at their place as they left.

If, however, the food tasted terrible and they did NOT enjoy the meal or the company, then they would carefully fold their napkin and set it to one side. This let everyone know they were NOT coming back again!

So when Jesus left the folded facecloth napkin, it was as if he were saying, "I will not come back here again!"

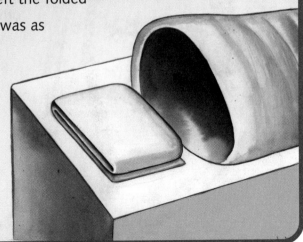

Mary Magdalene

Mary was from the tiny village called Magdala, on the western shore of the Sea of Galilee. In the book of Mark we read that Jesus had driven seven evil spirits out of Mary.

Mary was thankful for all Jesus had done for her. He had changed her life. She was one of the women who used her own money to help take care of Jesus as he traveled to different cities. She served him in every way she could.

This Sunday she brought Jesus her final offering—the spices she prepared for his body. When she saw the open grave, she immediately ran to find Peter and John.

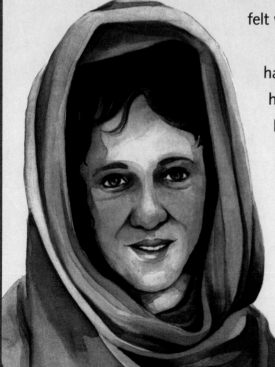

What sadness Mary must have felt when Jesus died. What joy she must have felt when she saw him alive! And Jesus honored Mary and the other women by appearing to them BEFORE he appeared to his disciples.

31

Is He Really Alive?

Matthew 28:8–10; Luke 24:9–12; John 20:2–10

When the women stepped out of the empty tomb, the words of the angel rang in their ears: "He is not here! He has risen, just as he said he would!"

Shaking with fear, they wondered if it was true. They rushed back to Jerusalem to find the disciples. They could hardly wait to tell the men what the angel had said. Their eyes sparkled with joy as they ran.

Suddenly Jesus stood in front of them. He smiled and said in a strong voice, "Greetings!"

The women stopped and blinked their eyes. It really was Jesus! They stepped closer to make sure. Then they fell down at his feet and worshiped him.

"Don't be afraid," Jesus said. "Go back and tell my brothers to go to Galilee. There they will see me."

As the women went into the city, Mary Magdalene finally arrived back at the tomb. But she found no one else there. Peter and John had just left.

Mary cried as she stooped down and looked inside the tomb. There she saw two angels dressed in white.

The angels were sitting beside the grave clothes where Jesus' body had been. One of them was sitting by the stone pillow where Jesus' head had been laid. The other angel sat where Jesus' feet had been.

The angels asked Mary, "Woman, why are you crying?"

"They have taken away my Lord," she said. "I don't know where they have put him."

Then Mary Magdalene turned around and saw Jesus standing there, but she didn't know who he was.

"Why are you crying?" he asked her. "Who are you looking for?"

Mary Magdalene thought Jesus was the gardener. So she said, "Sir, if you have taken his body away, please tell me. Then I will go and get him."

Then Jesus said to her, "Mary."

She knew that voice! It had to be Jesus! She looked closely and finally recognized him.

"Teacher!" she cried out.

"Don't hold on to me," Jesus said. "I haven't returned to the Father. But go tell my disciples that I am returning to my Father and my God, as well as your Father and your God."

Mary ran to find the other followers of Jesus. She told them, "I have seen the Lord!" But no one would believe anything she said.

Why didn't Mary Magdalene recognize Jesus?

Why do you think Jesus showed himself to Mary first?

Do you believe Jesus rose from the dead and is alive? Why?

"We know that God raised . . . Jesus from the dead. And he will also raise us up with Jesus. He will bring us . . . to God in heaven" (2 Corinthians 4:14).

Angels in Jesus' Life

Angels appeared during important events in Jesus' life.

An angel told Mary that she would be the mother of Jesus (Luke 1:26–38). An angel appeared to Joseph in a dream to tell him that Mary's baby was the Son of God (Matthew 1:18–25). An angel told the shepherds of Jesus' birth, and an angel choir sang God's praise (Luke 2:8–14).

An angel warned Joseph to leave Bethlehem because soldiers were coming to kill the baby boys. And some years later an angel came to Joseph in Egypt and told him to return to Israel (Matthew 2:13–22).

Angels strengthened Jesus in the wilderness and in the Garden of Gethsemane (Luke 22:43). Angels appeared when Jesus rose from the dead. And angels were there when Jesus went up in the clouds (Luke 24:1–7; Acts 1:10–11).

Two Followers Who Gave Up

Imagine how the disciples and other followers of Jesus felt after Jesus died. All their hopes and dreams of a Messiah had died, too. They were without their Master and Teacher for the first time in over three years.

The followers of Jesus knew they also could be arrested. Filled with fear, they hid behind locked doors after Jesus died on Friday. On Saturday, the Sabbath, they were unable to travel, so they remained in hiding.

But the next day, Sunday, they could travel again. So two followers of Jesus, Cleopas and a friend, decided to leave Jerusalem. They set out for their hometown of Emmaus, about seven miles away.

32

Sunday Afternoon: Heading Back Home

Luke 24:13–35

Cleopas and his friend walked together silently as they left the city and headed back to their hometown.

"I know the women said Jesus was alive, but I just can't believe it," Cleopas told his friend.

As they crossed over the brook, Jesus joined them on the path, but they didn't know who he was. God kept them from recognizing him.

Walking beside them, Jesus asked, "Why are you two men so sad and gloomy?"

Cleopas stared at him. "Are you the only person who doesn't know what has happened in Jerusalem?"

"Tell me about it," said Jesus with a smile.

Cleopas explained, "Jesus of Nazareth was a mighty prophet from God. We had hoped he would set our nation free. But our leaders arrested him and had him crucified. This morning some women went to his tomb. They came back and told us about the angels they saw. The angels told them that Jesus was alive."

"Some of the disciples ran to the tomb," said Cleopas. "They saw the empty burial cloths, but they didn't see Jesus."

Jesus asked them, "Why can't you understand? Why don't you believe what the prophets wrote? Didn't the Messiah sent from God have to suffer and die and come alive again?"

While they walked through the countryside, Jesus explained everything written about himself in the Scriptures. He began with Moses and all the Prophets.

All the time Jesus spoke, Cleopas felt a great joy fill his heart. But he still didn't recognize Jesus.

When they arrived at their village, Jesus acted as if he were going to walk farther down the road. But Cleopas begged him, "It is late. Stay and eat with us."

So Jesus followed them into the house. They prepared some food and sat down at the table to eat. As the guest of honor, Jesus took the bread, gave thanks, and broke it. Then he handed the bread to them.

At once Cleopas and his friend recognized him—the stranger was Jesus! But then Jesus suddenly disappeared.

Cleopas jumped up and shouted for joy, "He's alive! No wonder I felt so excited when he explained all the Scriptures! Let's run back to Jerusalem and tell the others!"

The two men raced back to the city. Cleopas couldn't hold back tears of joy that streamed down his face. *Jesus is alive!* he thought as he ran. *It's a miracle! But I wonder if any of the disciples will believe what happened.*

What did Jesus explain to Cleopas and his friend?

Why did Cleopas and his friend run back to Jerusalem?

Why can we be sure Jesus is the Savior of whom the prophets spoke?

"The LORD's servant took the sins of many people on himself. And he gave his life for those who had done what is wrong" (Isaiah 53:12).

What Prophecies Came True?

Jesus is the only man who ever lived who has fulfilled every prophecy written about the coming Messiah.

1. The Messiah would be born of an unmarried woman (Genesis 3:15; Isaiah 7:14).
2. The Messiah would come from King David (2 Samuel 7:12, 13, 16).
3. The Messiah would be born in Bethlehem. (Micah 5:2).
4. The Messiah would be presented with gifts (Psalm 72:10; Isaiah 60:3, 6).
5. The Messiah would begin his work in Galilee (Isaiah 9:1–2).
6. The Messiah would enter Jerusalem on a donkey (Zechariah 9:9).
7. The Messiah would be betrayed by a friend (Psalm 41:9).
8. The Messiah would be sold for thirty pieces of silver (Zechariah 11:12–13).
9. The Messiah would be wounded and pierced (Psalm 22:14–16; Zechariah 12:10).
10. The Messiah would be mocked and hated (Psalm 22:6–8; Isaiah 53:3).
11. The Messiah would die with sinners (Isaiah 53:9).
12. The Messiah would be buried in a rich man's grave (Isaiah 53:9, 12).
13. The Messiah would rise from the dead (Psalm 16:8–11; 30:3; 41:10; Hosea 6:1–2).

Behind Locked Doors

Many people followed Jesus. Some of them, like the twelve disciples, had been with him for over three years.

At one time Jesus sent out seventy-two of his followers (Luke 10:1–23). They went to every town ahead of Jesus. Their job was to help get people ready for his visit.

When they came back from their trips, they gave some exciting reports. "Lord, even the demons obey us when we speak in your name" (Luke 10:17).

Many of these followers may have been hiding behind locked doors with the disciples on Sunday. Not one of the disciples or followers seemed to believe Jesus' words that he would rise from the dead on the third day.

33

Sunday Evening: Is It a Ghost?

Luke 24:33–49; John 20:19–23

Peter looked up as someone pounded loudly on the door of the house where he and the other disciples were staying. *Is it our turn to be arrested?* he wondered.

"Let us in!" called a familiar voice. "We have good news to tell you!"

"It's Cleopas," Peter told the others as he unbolted the door and let the two friends come inside. "What a surprise!" said Peter. "I thought you both went back to your hometown this morning."

Cleopas laughed. "We did! But we met a stranger who walked with us on the road and explained all the Scriptures to us. And now we finally understand! Jesus IS the suffering servant Isaiah wrote about. Jesus IS the promised Messiah!

"When we got to our home, we invited the stranger to stay and eat with us. When he prayed over the bread and handed it to us, we finally recognized him! It was Jesus! But immediately he disappeared!"

While Peter was listening to Cleopas explain all that had happened, suddenly Jesus stood beside him.

Jesus said to all of them, "May peace be with you!"

Peter felt shocked and terrified. *Am I seeing a ghost?* he wondered. *Is it really Jesus?*

"Why are you upset and afraid?" asked Jesus. "Why do you have doubts in your minds? Look at my hands and my feet. It is really I! Touch me and see."

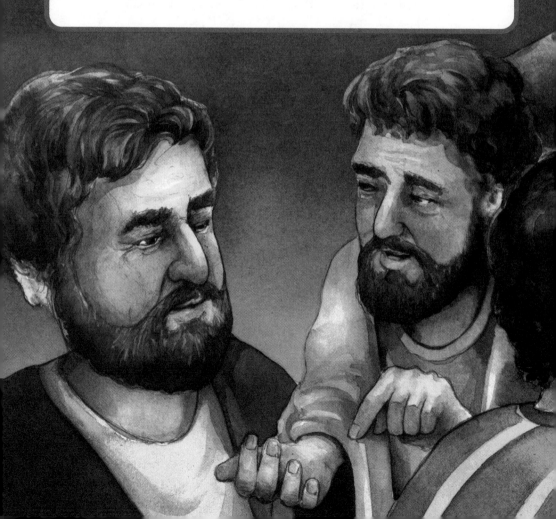

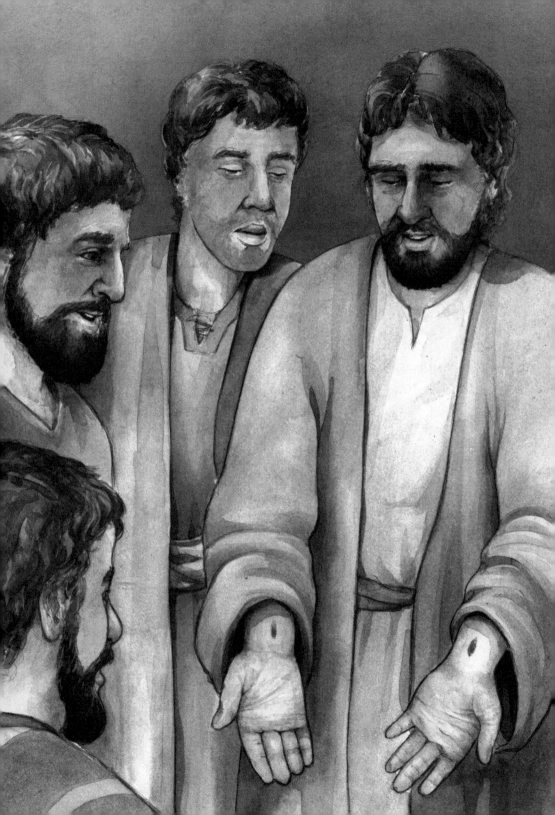

"A ghost does not have a body or bones. But you can see that I do," Jesus said. He smiled as he looked around at their shocked faces. For once Peter was speechless.

"Do you have anything here to eat?" Jesus asked.

Peter handed him a piece of cooked fish and some honeycomb. Jesus took it and ate it while they watched.

Jesus isn't a ghost, thought Peter. *He has a real body.*

"This is what I told you before," said Jesus. "All that is written about me in the Law of Moses, the Prophets, and the Psalms must come true." Then Jesus explained everything and helped them understand the Scriptures.

"The Father has sent me," he said. "Now I am sending you. For now, stay here in Jerusalem until you receive power from heaven. I am going to send you what my Father has promised—the Holy Spirit."

Why were the disciples afraid when they saw Jesus?

How do you think Jesus got into the locked room?

What kind of body will you have someday in heaven?

(Read Philippians 3:20–21).

"I know that my Redeemer lives. In the end he will stand on the earth. After my skin has been destroyed, in my body I'll still see God. I myself will see him with my own eyes" (Job 19:25–27).

Jesus' New Body

When Jesus rose from the dead, he made sure that his followers knew he was real. He invited them to touch him. And he ate some fish while they watched. Then they knew he was not a ghost. Whoever heard of a ghost eating food?

But what kind of body did Jesus have? It was still a physical body that could be seen and touched. But the wounds in his hands and feet were completely healed, leaving only scars

With this new body, Jesus had gone out of the tomb without ever moving the stone. And he went through locked doors without opening them. His body appeared and disappeared right before people's eyes.

Even though he looked the same, Jesus had a new body— a body that would never die again.

Thomas Didymus

Think of all the disciples who followed Jesus. Who is the one known as the "doubter"? It is Thomas. He was the one who needed more proof to believe Jesus was alive.

He also seemed to be the disciple who was the most pessimistic and gloomy. Once Jesus told his disciples that Lazarus was dead and that he was going to go to Bethany. So Thomas said to the rest of the disciples, "Let us go also. Then we can die with Jesus" (John 11:16).

Tradition tells us that Thomas traveled further east to share the good news of Jesus in Syria, Persia, and India.

34

Sunday, One Week Later: Give Me Proof!

John 20:24–29

Thomas was the only one of the eleven remaining disciples of Jesus who was not there on Sunday night when Jesus appeared.

When he saw the other ten disciples later, they told him, "We have seen the Lord! He is really alive! He has risen from the dead!"

That's impossible, thought Thomas. He frowned and shook his head, unable to believe their report.

"First I must see the nail marks in his hands," he said. "I must put my finger where the nails were. I must put my hand into his side. Only then will I ever believe what you say."

Then, a week later, Jesus' disciples all met together in the house again. This time Thomas was with them.

Even though the doors were shut and locked, Jesus suddenly came and stood in the middle of the room. Now Thomas saw Jesus with his own eyes.

Jesus smiled as he looked around at each of his followers. No one said a word.

"May peace be with you!" said Jesus.

Then Jesus turned and looked directly at Thomas. He reached out his hand and said to him, "Put your finger here where the nails have been. See my hands. Reach out your hand and put it into my side."

The other disciples were silent. Thomas knew they were grinning as they watched him.

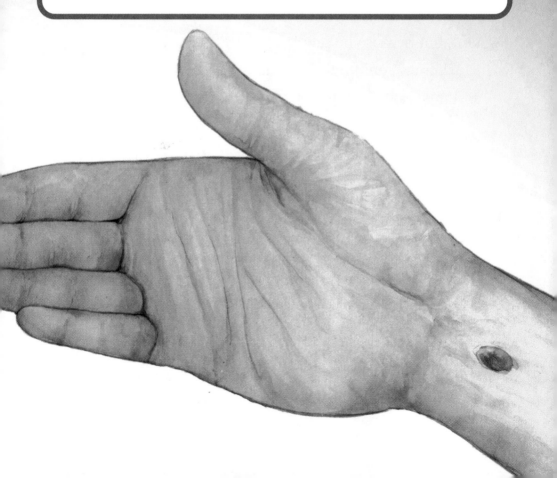

Thomas didn't know what to believe. Was he seeing things? Did Jesus really come in through a locked door?

"Stop doubting, Thomas," Jesus said gently. "Believe that I am alive."

Overcome with joy, all Thomas could do was fall to his knees in front of Jesus. Thomas didn't reach out his finger to touch the hands or feet of Jesus. He didn't put his hand into the wound he saw in Jesus' side. He didn't have to—now he believed. He knew he was seeing the risen, living Jesus. Now he believed, not because of what the others said, but because he saw Jesus with his own eyes.

Thomas could only say one thing. "You are my Lord and my God!" he told Jesus.

Then Jesus said to him, "Because you have seen me, Thomas, you have believed. Blessed are those who have not seen me, but have still believed in me."

Why wouldn't Thomas believe the reports that Jesus was alive?
Why didn't Thomas touch Jesus' hands and feet?
Will you trust and believe in Jesus without seeing him?

"Faith is being sure of what we hope for. It is being certain of what we do not see" (Hebrews 11:1).

Doubters, Liars, and Believers

What different kinds of reactions did people have when Jesus rose from the dead?

1. <u>Selfishness</u>—The Roman guards worried about themselves. They wanted to make sure they weren't punished for failing their assigned duties.

2. <u>Denial</u>—The priests and Pharisees didn't want to hear the truth. Then they asked the guards to lie about what had happened.

3. <u>Joy</u>—The women sadly brought their spices to the tomb. They left with great joy!

4. <u>Skepticism</u>—Peter ran to the tomb, looked in at the grave clothes, and wondered what happened.

5. <u>Unbelief</u>—None of the disciples believed the report brought by Mary Magdalene and the women.

6. <u>Doubt</u>—Thomas refused to believe the other disciples. He wanted proof.

7. <u>Amazement and faith</u>—Thomas finally believed after he saw Jesus with his own eyes.

Fishermen at Work

Peter, Andrew, James, and John had all been fishermen at the Sea of Galilee before they followed Jesus. Most of the time, they fished during the night. It was easier to catch fish at night. That is when fish come out of their hiding places to feed. And they can't see the nets in the dark.

Peter probably used a dragnet for fishing. It was a large net with floats on the upper edge and weights on the lower edge. Weights helped the net go deep into the lake.

After Jesus' resurrection, the disciples left Jerusalem. They returned to their homes around the Sea of Galilee. Jesus had said he would meet them in Galilee. Fishing became their job again. They knew Jesus was alive, but perhaps they were wondering what to do next.

35

Sometime Later: Fishing Again

John 21:1–14

One evening Peter and six other disciples went to the Sea of Galilee. Peter pulled one of his father's boats out into the water and climbed in. "I'm going out to fish," he told the others.

"We'll go with you," they said. So they all got in the boat. Peter rowed the boat away from the shore. They fished all night, but they didn't catch anything.

Early in the morning, Peter saw a man standing on the shore. He asked John, "Who is that man?"

"I don't know," said John.

"Friends, don't you have any fish?" called the man.

"No," Peter and the others called back.

The man called out to them, "Throw your net on the right side of the boat. There you'll find some fish."

"What?" said Peter. "That doesn't make sense. How could there be fish on the other side of our boat?"

"Oh, come on, Peter," said John. "Let's try. Help us throw the net out on the other side. It won't hurt us to do what the man says."

When Peter helped throw the net over on the other side of the boat, a great number of fish instantly filled it!

"What is happening?" asked Peter as he tried to hang on to the heavy net. He yanked at the net, trying to pull it into the boat, but it was too full of fish!

John grabbed his arm and said, "It's the Lord!"

As soon as Peter heard John's words, he knew the man on shore was Jesus. He jumped into the water and swam to shore. He couldn't wait to talk to Jesus.

Peter sat close to Jesus by a fire of burning coals. They talked together while Jesus cooked some fish on the fire. Finally the rest of the disciples reached the shore, towing the net full of fish behind their boat.

When the boat landed, Jesus called out to them, "Bring some of the fish you just caught."

Jumping up, Peter ran to the boat and helped the other men drag the net to shore. He checked over the net right away to see if it had been ripped. Then he helped count all the fish.

"I can hardly believe there were 153 fish in the net," he said. "Why didn't the net rip from the heavy load?"

"Come and have breakfast," Jesus said to them. He handed them bread and fish and they all ate.

This was the third time Jesus appeared to his disciples after he had risen from the dead.

How did John know who was on shore?

Why did Peter swim to shore instead of staying in the boat?

When have you spent time alone with Jesus?

"If we admit that we have sinned . . . God will forgive every wrong thing we have done" (1 John 1:9).

Do You Love Me?

When they finished eating the fish, Jesus called Peter by his real name. "Simon, son of John," said Jesus, "do you truly love me more than these others do?"

"Yes, Lord," Peter answered. "You know that I love you."

Jesus said to him, "Feed my lambs." Then Jesus asked Peter the same question again. "Simon, do you love me?"

Peter answered, "Yes, Lord. You know that I love you."

Jesus said, "Take care of my sheep." And he asked Peter a third time, "Simon, son of John, do you love me?"

Peter felt bad because Jesus asked the question for the third time. He said, "Lord, you know all things. You know that I love you." Peter had denied Jesus three times. Now he declared his love for Jesus three times (John 21:15–17).

Living Proof!

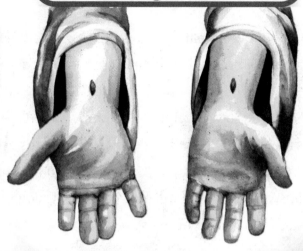

During the forty days after his death and resurrection, Jesus proved many times that he was alive. He appeared to people at least ten different times after his resurrection.

One time five hundred people saw him at once. Everyone saw the wounds in his hands and feet—the living proof of his resurrection from the dead.

During these appearances, Jesus often spoke to his followers about the kingdom of God.

One day while eating with his friends, Jesus gave this command: "Do not leave Jerusalem yet. Wait here for my Father to give you the gift he promised—the Holy Spirit. You have heard me talk about it [John 14:15–17, 25–26; 17:5–15]. John baptized with water. But in a few days you will be baptized with the Holy Spirit" (Acts 1:1–5).

36

Forty Days Later: Up in the Clouds

Acts 1:1–11

On the fortieth day after his resurrection, Jesus and his disciples met at the top of the Mount of Olives.

Peter asked Jesus, "Lord, are you going to give the kingdom back to Israel now?"

"You don't need to know the time of those events," said Jesus. "Only the Father knows."

Jesus promised, "You will receive power when the Holy Spirit comes upon you. Then you will be my witnesses. You will tell everybody in Jerusalem, in all of Israel, and everywhere in the world about me."

After Jesus said this, he was lifted up from the middle of the disciples, where he had been standing.

Peter's mouth fell open when he saw Jesus rise up higher and higher in the sky. *What is Jesus doing now?* he wondered. He couldn't say a word as Jesus rose up toward heaven. And he didn't take his eyes off Jesus until he was taken up into a cloud.

Even after the cloud hid Jesus from their sight, Peter and the disciples still wouldn't leave the top of the mountain. They just kept standing there and looking up into the sky.

Suddenly Peter was startled to see two men dressed in white clothing standing beside them.

The strangers asked the disciples, "Why do you men of Galilee stand here looking at the sky? Jesus has been taken away from you into heaven. But he will come back again in the same way you have seen him go."

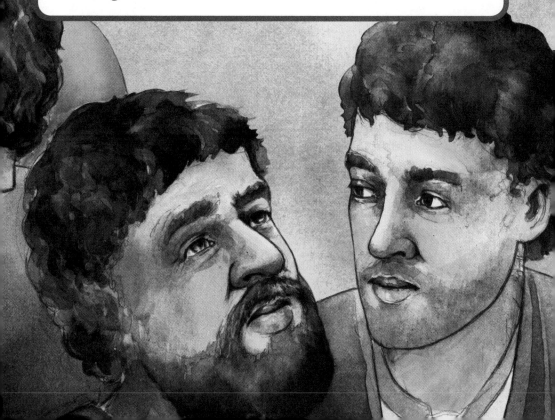

Peter finally headed down the Mount of Olives with the other disciples. He couldn't stop talking about what had happened as they walked back to Jerusalem, which was about a mile away.

They returned to the upstairs room where they had been staying. This was probably the same room where Jesus had celebrated the Last Supper with them.

For the next ten days, Peter and the disciples, along with other followers of Jesus, prayed, sang praise, and worshiped God with all their heart.

About 120 believers came together every day for prayer and worship. Many women were also part of this group, as were Mary, the mother of Jesus, and the brothers of Jesus. They must have all wondered, *When will the Holy Spirit come? What kind of "power" will he give us? And how long will we have to wait?*

What was the message of the two angels?

How do you think the people felt when they saw Jesus leave?

What do you think it will be like to see Jesus return to earth?

"Jesus said, 'And you can be sure that I am always with you, to the very end'" (Matthew 28:20).

The Ten-Day Wait

"Wait for the gift my Father promised." These were some of the last words that Jesus spoke to his followers.

About 120 men and women met together in the Upper Room day after day for the next ten days. They waited for God's gift of the Holy Spirit. They weren't quite sure what was going to happen or how long it would take.

As they waited, they ate together, prayed together, and talked with each other. They probably couldn't stop talking about Jesus' death, resurrection, and ascension.

Each of them may have shared how they first met Jesus. Maybe they laughed about good memories of Jesus. During this time Matthias was chosen to take the place of Judas as one of the twelve disciples.

Most of all, everyone patiently waited. That's what Jesus had told them to do.

Feast of Pentecost

The great Feast of Pentecost was celebrated each year on the fiftieth day after Passover.

Jewish believers traveled to Jerusalem from all over the world to thank God for their harvest. At this time, people celebrated their barley harvest by bringing gifts of the first barley grains to God. They also brought the first loaves of bread made from this grain.

Ten days before this feast, Jesus had ascended into heaven. He promised his disciples, "In a few days you will be baptized with the Holy Spirit" (Acts 1:5).

After his ascension, all of the believers met together and prayed every day. The tenth day on which they met for prayer was the beginning of the Feast of Pentecost.

37

Pentecost Morning:
The Gift Arrives!

Acts 2:1–40

On Sunday morning, seven weeks after Jesus rose from the dead, the disciples were gathered together. Suddenly Peter heard the sound of a strong wind. It came from heaven and filled the house where they were meeting.

Peter opened his eyes to see what was happening. Everyone else looked around, too. They watched in amazement as something that looked like tongues of fire came down on their heads. The flames separated and settled on each of the men and women. And they were all filled with the Holy Spirit.

Peter found himself speaking in a strange language he had not known before. So did the others. Full of joy, they praised God with loud voices.

But soon Peter heard voices of people who were outside their house of prayer. Peter went out to see them.

The crowds who were visiting Jerusalem heard the sound of the wind. They came outside and looked around, trying to find out what was happening.

The crowd of visitors told Peter, "We heard the sound of a great wind. We wanted to find out what it was."

When Peter and the others began speaking in many different languages, the crowd felt confused.

"We are from all over the world," they said. "How can all of you speak to us in many different languages? Why do we all hear you talking about the wonderful things God has done?"

The visitors from many countries were amazed. "What does this mean?" they asked each other.

But some people made fun of the believers and said, "They've had too much wine to drink!"

Peter spoke in a loud voice so everyone could hear. "You are wrong to think all of these people are drunk. They aren't. It is only nine o'clock in the morning. But this is what was spoken of by the prophet Joel."

Peter told the crowd, "God said, 'In the last days, I will give my Holy Spirit to everyone. In those days I will pour out my Spirit on those who serve me—your sons and daughters, both men and women.'"

"You nailed Jesus to the cross," said Peter. "But God raised him up. God has given him a place of honor in heaven. Now Jesus has given the Holy Spirit to us. That is what you are seeing and hearing."

Immediately the people felt ashamed and upset. They asked Peter, "What should we do?"

"Turn back to God," Peter answered. "Be baptized in the name of Jesus Christ. Then your sins will be forgiven. And you will receive the gift of the Holy Spirit. For the promise is for you and your children."

Those who accepted Peter's message were baptized— about three thousand of them!

What happened to Jesus' followers on Pentecost?

How were people different after being filled with the Holy Spirit?

Have you asked God to give you the gift of his Holy Spirit?

"Turn away from your sins and be baptized in the name of Jesus Christ. Then your sins will be forgiven. You will receive the gift of the Holy Spirit" (Acts 2:38).

First Christian Community

When people received the gift of the Holy Spirit, they were changed! Now the disciples boldly told people about Jesus' death and resurrection. They spoke with great power. And they were not afraid of anyone.

Miracles of healing took place every day. Many people were saved. The church grew and grew and grew.

The believers shared everything they owned with each other. They met every day to pray and praise God. They loved each other. Their hearts were glad and honest and true. They were respected by all of the people.

There were no needy persons among this first Christian community. Everyone willingly sold their land or houses and brought the money to be shared with anyone who needed it (Acts 2:42–47; 4:32–35).

Decision Time for YOU

It Was for YOU

Now you know all about the final events of Jesus' life. You've read about his resurrection, his appearances after his resurrection, his ascension into heaven, and the coming of the promised Holy Spirit.

It's great that you now know all the facts. But Jesus doesn't want you to just know ABOUT him. He wants you to KNOW him! He wants you to put your whole trust in him. He wants to save you.

Remember in the story how the curtain in the Temple split from top to bottom? Remember that it was a sign that Jesus had opened the door right into God's presence? Remember that his death made a way for us to go to heaven?

Now all that is left is for you to believe Jesus died for you. All you have to do is trust that he is alive and with you today. All you have to do is ask his forgiveness for your sin. Everything Jesus did, he did for you. Now he is offering you his gifts of love, forgiveness, and eternal life.

"Believe in the Lord Jesus.
Then you and your family will be saved"
(Acts 16:31).

Will You Believe the Witnesses?

1. Judges and juries usually believe a witness who testifies, especially if the person had been an "eyewitness." Can you believe and trust what the disciples said they saw with their own eyes?

2. Will you believe what the disciples wrote about Jesus? Much more happened that the gospel writers of Matthew, Mark, Luke, and John didn't even write down.
   John tells us, "Jesus also did many other things. What if every one of them were written down? I suppose that even the whole world would not have room for the books that would be written" (John 21:25).

3. Over five hundred people saw Jesus alive during the forty days following his resurrection before he went up into heaven. Some of those people were:

   Mary Magdalene,

   Joanna, Mary (the mother of James) and

   Salome and other women who went to the tomb,

   Simon Peter,

   two followers on the road to Emmaus,

   ten disciples in the Upper Room,

   ten disciples and Thomas (one week later),

   five hundred who people saw him at once,

   seven disciples at the Sea of Galilee,

   the eleven disciples and others who witnessed his ascension forty days after Passover.

4. Peter wrote these words: "We told you about the time our Lord Jesus Christ came with power. But we didn't make up stories when we told you about it. With our own eyes we saw him in all his majest." (2 Peter 1:16).

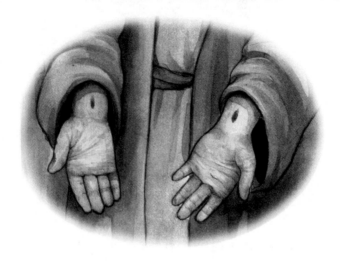

Will You Trust That He Is Alive?

Remember the HISTORICAL EVIDENCE of Jesus' resurrection:

1. The Roman seal was broken and the gravestone was moved far away from the hillside. Everyone who looked inside the tomb saw the empty grave clothes. Everyone saw that Jesus' body was gone.

2. Jesus' body could not have been pulled out of the cloths without the cloths being unwrapped. Any powdered spices that had not hardened would have spilled all over the floor. Any hardened ointment would have become like glue, making it nearly impossible to unwind the cloths.

3. The disciples could not have stolen his body. They were too scared. And why would they want to steal it? Why would they want to tell lies about Jesus being alive? After they did tell others that Jesus was alive, they only got into more trouble with the Jewish leaders.

4. No one ever found the bones or the dead body of Jesus. If Jesus did NOT come alive, then where was his body? A dead body can't be hidden for very long.

5. If the disciples DID steal the body of Jesus, both they and the guards should have been punished. If the guards were asleep while the body was stolen, didn't they deserve to be put to death, as the law required?

6. Think of how the cowardly disciples changed after Jesus rose from the dead! They turned into bold witnesses who went everywhere telling people about Jesus. Neither threats of prison nor death stopped them. What made them change? Were they telling the truth . . . or a lie? If they were lying, why were they willing to die for their lies?

It's Time to Decide

See him standing in Pilate's hall.
See him forsaken, betrayed by all.
Listen—he sends you an urgent call.
Now what will you do about Jesus?

Please don't evade him as Pilate tried.
Please choose to obey him and walk by his side.
Please don't run away from him, trying to hide.
Please think what you'll do about Jesus.

Have you, like Peter, your Lord denied?
Have you sinned and his patience tried?
When you've disobeyed, have you wept and cried?
Think now what you'll do about Jesus.

"Dear Jesus, I give you my heart today!
I'm willing to follow you all of the way.
Your voice, dear Lord, I will gladly obey."
I know what I'll do about Jesus!

You Have a Choice

1. Accept Jesus as your Savior.
   Follow him.
   Receive his love and the gifts he offers.

2. Or reject him and live your life apart from him.
   That would be the worst tragedy that could happen.

"We love because he loved us first" (1 John 4:19).

If you want to give your life to Jesus right now, you can pray this prayer:

Thank you, Lord Jesus.
I believe you died for my sin.
I believe you rose from the dead.
I accept your gift of love.
Forgive me all of my sins.
I give myself to you.
I give my whole life to you.
And I trust you as my Savior.
Come and live with me.
I want to follow you and live for you always.
Fill me with your Holy Spirit.
Thank you, Jesus.
Amen.

"God chose us to belong to Christ
before the world was created.
He loved us. So he decided long ago
to adopt us as his children.
He did it because of what Jesus Christ had done"
(Ephesians 1:4–5)

If you prayed this prayer to Jesus,
sign your name here:

Name_____

Date_____

This is the most important day of your life.
You have been adopted as a child of God.
This is like your second birthday.
Remember this day always.

Jesus loves you!
And don't you ever doubt it!

"May you have power with all God's people
to understand Christ's love.
May you know how wide and long
and high and deep it is.
And may you know his love,
even though it can't be known completely.
Then you will be filled with everything
God has for you"
(Ephesians 3:18-19).

DICTIONARY
of Words Used in This book

Apostle—Someone Jesus chose to teach others about him.

Christ—The Greek word for "Messiah: or the "Anointed One."

Covenant—A treaty between two persons or groups in which promises are made.

Crucify—to put people to death by nailing them on a cross.

Disciple—A pupil. Someone who learns from a teacher and imitates the teacher.

Israel—Hebrew word meaning "God strives" or "God rules." The nation that came from the twelve sons of Jacob (God changed Jacob's name to Israel in Genesis 32:28).

Jerusalem—The capital and the most important city in Israel. The Temple for sacrifice and worship was built here.

Jews—A name for people who were born of the twelve sons of Jacob.

Messiah—A Hebrew word meaning "the Anointed One." The Messiah was to save or redeem the people of Israel from their enemies. Prophets of old foretold the birth of the Messiah.

Miracle—Something very special and wonderful that only can be done by God.

Mount of Olives—A mountain east of Jerusalem where olive trees grew.

Passover—The most important Jewish feast, celebrating the Jews' deliverance from Egyptian slavery.

Pentecost—A feast that was celebrated fifty days after Passover.

Pharisees—The largest and most influential religious-political party during New Testament times.

Priest—One who served in the Temple and offered his own, as well as other people's sacrifices to God.

Prophet—One who speaks for God and declares God's word.

Prophecy—A spoken or written word given by God to people.

Resurrection—The event of being brought back from death to a life that never ends.

Roman Empire—The international rule of the Roman government over Israel and other countries.

Sacrifice—A gift offered to God as a gift of thanks or a sin offering. Perfect young bulls, cows, lambs, goats, pigeons, and turtledoves were brought to God.

Sanhedrin—The seventy-member Jewish court of law. The most important Jewish court in Jesus' time.

Savior—One who saves. A person who sets people free from their sin.

Scriptures—The books of history, the Psalms, and the writings of Moses and the prophets of the Old Testament.

Temple—A word meaning "holy place." A place built for worship and as a symbol of God's presence among people.

Tomb—A place to bury dead bodies. It was often a cave.